DONALD O. RICKTER
(at Arlington Street Church,
Boston, 15 Dec. 1974)

With very best wishes,

Marie Buckley

9 Feb '75

BREAKING INTO PRISON

Photo by Mason Morfit

BREAKING INTO PRISON

A Citizen Guide to
Volunteer Action

by Marie Buckley

Beacon Press   Boston

To the unknown volunteers who hold the key
to meaningful change

Beacon Press books are published under the auspices
of the Unitarian Universalist Association

Published simultaneously in Canada by Saunders of Toronto, Ltd.

Printed in the United States of America

9 8 7 6 5 4 3 2 1

Library of Congress Cataloging in Publication Data

Buckley, Marie.
    Breaking into prison.
    Bibliography:
    1. Volunteer workers in corrections—United States.
I. Title.
HV9304.B83   365′.66   74–206
ISBN 0–8070–0876–1

CONTENTS

Part II   OUTSIDE THE WALLS

ACKNOWLEDGMENTS

There are at least a hundred people who have contributed in one way or another to this book. They include prison administrators, guards, and inmates, judges and probation officers, policemen and victims of crime, and many, many volunteers with whom I spent countless hours in conversation. To all of them I am thankful.

However, there are a few people who played such critical roles that I extend to them very special thanks:

Harvard Law School's Center for Criminal Justice has my lasting gratitude for several reasons. The law school provided me with a base for research and writing during nearly two academic years. The staff helped me make countless contacts with programs and professionals in all parts of the country. Professors who included me in their criminal justice seminars taught me most of what I know about the dynamics of the system. By providing me with every facility I could possibly require, Harvard also eliminated my usual reasons for procrastination.

Professors James Vorenberg, Lloyd Ohlin, and Walter Miller have been particularly responsible for this work because of their criticism, reassurance, patience, and inspiration. They did not know it at the time, but during moments when I felt I could not finish the book, one factor which spurred me on was my desire not to violate the trust they had shown by encouraging this work.

The other person without whom the book would not have been produced is John J. Buckley, Sheriff of Middlesex County, in Massachusetts, who is clearly the country's most creative prison administrator (and who also happens to be my spouse). It was he who first introduced me to the prison world, who is the source of many stories in this book, and who gets credit for the title.

He is both a source of and a sounding board for ideas, my first reader of rough drafts, and my severest critic. But he is also my most loyal supporter, my catalyst when everything grinds to a halt, and the continuing strength and joy of my life.

My brother, Harry Costello, pricked my social conscience by suggesting that what was stored in my head ought to be shared with others for a useful purpose. That conversation was the beginning of the book.

Jarvis Jennings, who taught me all the prison slang and con tricks I know, is almost entirely responsible for the glossary in this book.

Finally, the National Center for Voluntary Action in Washington and the National Center for Volunteers in Courts in Boulder were most helpful sources of information and cross-checking on the voluntary programs which I was unable to observe personally.

PREFACE

Some years ago, a small group of ex-inmates was developing an experimental program at the Massachusetts Correctional Institution at Norfolk, Massachusetts, through which they were preparing to counsel inmates. They wanted an outsider to serve as an objective observer of the program and to keep a written record of its progress. That's where I came in: to write the report. And, having done so, that's where I intended to leave the prison scene. However, in 1970, my husband became Sheriff of Middlesex County, Massachusetts, and took charge of a prison which had never seen a volunteer or a program of any kind. I found it impossible to turn my back when the needs were so obvious and extensive, and the workers so few. My first job was to start a library; then to help recruit volunteers; and finally to assist in launching what is now a full-blown volunteer program.

Frequent public-speaking opportunities began during my husband's campaign. And, everywhere I went, people asked the same basic questions: what is prison like; what are the prisoners like; how can we help to change conditions; how do we get in; what do we need to know before we go? I looked for a book which would answer these questions, and to my surprise, found no appropriate materials. So, I finally decided to write the book myself.

Since prison conditions vary widely from place to place and time to time, it is impossible to tell any reader *exactly* what to expect in his own locality. This book is designed to give you an overview of conditions you are most likely to encounter; to show the close relationship between society and those it castigates; and to suggest ways in which our responsibilities to our own criminal justice system, and those involved in it, can be met both inside and outside the prison walls.

PART I

INSIDE THE WALLS

Item: New York Times, *December 12, 1971*

Little Rock, Arkansas—Willie Stewart, a skinny black youth convicted of burglary, arrived at Cummins Prison Farm before dawn on November 29 to serve a one-day sentence that was supposed to show him the bleakness of a life of crime.

After a day of hazing by prison guards and inmate trusties and of hard work in the prison cotton field, the 17-year-old boy lost consciousness and died on the way to a hospital. . . .

OF PRISONS
AND
PRISONERS

Item: Boston Globe, *August 20, 1973*

Malden, Massachusetts—Several hundred relatives, friends and longtime customers went yesterday to Temple Tifereth Israel to pay their last respects to Hyman Gordon, a druggist for 42 years.

The 62-year-old Gordon, of East Border Road, was shot to death Friday morning while attempting to stop an armed robbery of his drug store, the Judson Square Pharmacy. . . .

Note: The accused murderer has been apprehended. He has a police and prison record of twelve years, dating from the time he was twenty-one years old. He has been in jail at least four times that we know of and has served two prison sentences.

These, admittedly, are the more sensational kinds of crime that we read about in newspapers every day of the year. We don't hear about the majority of our prisons, where open physical violence is not generally indulged in. We don't hear about the majority of crimes, which are not violent crimes. This is unfortunate because it means we fail to gain knowledge about what ordinary prisons, and ordinary criminals are like. We thus fail to see the nonphysical, more insidious violence that is done to the spirit of a nation.

There are continuing incidents of violence and brutality visited upon the helpless. The shocking part, beyond the violence itself, is that it exists not only on the streets, but within the very system we have designed to prevent it. As rational human beings, we have to abhor violence wherever we find it, and our sympathies must be extended to all its victims whether they come from our own hometown or from the state prison. As responsible citizens as well as decent human beings, we have an obligation to do what we can to prevent crime and injustice. Clearly, we cannot eliminate all crime and violence, but as citizens we can help to change our system of criminal justice so that the system itself does not contribute to the violence. We have an obligation, like the ancient Greeks, to leave the society and its institutions a little better than we found them.

It may be a significant mark of modern American civilization that we increasingly perceive a certain guilt for wrongdoing in our institutions as well as in individuals. We are more and more aware of scandals in our system which contribute to the cycle of crime and violence we abhor. The scandals are that the law has favored some groups over others, that justice is unequal for rich and for poor, that prisons create as much crime as they correct, and that society's revenge on the criminals it catches is often more cruel than the original crime.

Meaningful change in our system cannot be achieved by a few isolated citizens, no matter how great their dedication. But many citizens working in concert do have the power to correct the scandals of our criminal justice system. To do something about them, we must have a certain knowledge of the system. Of all our institutions, the most difficult to know and to penetrate is the prison, the most remote part of the system. But let us look at the little that can be seen of it.

Not only are prisons remote from ordinary scrutiny so that we are never sure, as citizens, exactly what occurs inside, but we even have difficulty finding what would seem like relatively simple facts. After considerable digging, I am not yet certain how many prisons there are in this country or how many people are in them. No one else is sure either, and there are several reasons for our lack of information.

The first is that, in a country as vast as the United States, with so many levels of government, there is no uniform system of reporting such facts to any central source. The federal government has one system; various states have others; and local governments which bother to report at all have still other systems.[1]

A second major problem in counting is a problem of semantics. For example, I may say that there are thirty-eight federal prisons. Someone from the Justice Department immediately will scream, "No. We have only six penitentiaries, three reformatories, ten correctional institutions, and . . ." Someone from a state system will say, "We don't have nine prisons. We have six prisons and three camps which are run by the prison department." Again: "We really only have one prison. The other institutions listed are community treatment centers." Personnel in the system become very incensed over such matters, and everyone wants a correctional center rather than a prison, as though changing the names made the slightest difference in the reality.

In spite of the dangers, I shall plunge ahead and say that we have thirty-eight federal prisons, approximately three hundred or so state prisons (depending on which you count as prisons), and something over four thousand local jails and county prisons.[2]

I use qualifying terms because I'm sure there are institutions we don't even know of. For example, when the President's Commission on Law Enforcement and the Administration of Justice surveyed the local institutions in 1965, they counted just over three thousand. By 1970, when a National Jail Census was done, over four thousand were counted.[3] Even then, only thirty-three of the fifty states reported in time or with sufficient information to allow inclusion of their data in the final count.

If the federal Department of Justice can't be sure how many prisons we have, I feel justified in giving approximate figures. In any case, it adds up to enough prisons, most likely, to cover the whole state of Texas, if we could put them wall to wall. And that does not include local police lockups, which have never been counted.

We are as unsure of the exact number of prisoners as we are the number of prisons, but I believe there are in the vicinity of 400,000 people in prison on any given day of the year: about 20,000 in federal institutions, some 193,000 in state facilities, and more than 160,000 in local jails and prisons. Again, this does not include *all* local prisoners, and my guess is that the local figure would go up to 200,000 if we could get accurate statistics.

Of these prisoners, the majority, about 325,000, are male adults. Another 20,000 or so are female adults. And we don't know how many juveniles are imprisoned, since the definition of juvenile varies from state to state. In some it is anyone under sixteen; in others, under eighteen; and in some, under twenty-one. And the semantics of what constitutes a prison are even worse on the juvenile level than on the adult, as you will see in a later chapter.

Multiply these approximate figures by three to include the number of offenders who are on probation or parole, or who are among the uncounted in halfway houses or camps or juvenile "homes." All in all, the total comes to over a million souls, more than enough to fill Boston and San Francisco combined.

Those who are in prison serve sentences which vary from less than one year to life. The sentences vary depending on the offense, the temperament of the judge, and the parole policies of the state. The vast majority of prisoners serve sentences of five years or less, but a very significant number serve more than that. It is not in the least bit unusual to meet a prisoner serving ten or twenty years, or life.

In 1970, of the some 4,600 new prisoners who came from court in California, nearly 2,000 had life sentences. In Ohio, out of 3,900 new prisoners, 1,778 received sentences of twenty years or more. In Washington State, one-third of its new prisoners were sentenced to eleven to twenty years. In the United States, prison sentences are among the longest to be found in any part of the Western world. The length of sentence plus the conditions of incarceration add up to a very unhealthy situation. Keep in mind always that about 97 percent of all persons in prison today are coming back to us in a few years. Pure self-interest, if nothing else, should lead us to the conclusion that what happens to them in prison is very important to all of us. Perhaps the Malden druggist would be alive today had one of the prisons given more effective treatment to his accused murderer.

Whether it is a vast federal penitentiary or a local pokey run on a shoestring, prisoners enter what is known as a total institution. A total institution is one which controls all aspects of a person's life. Every activity is conducted in the same place, directed by the same authority, and performed in a strictly ordered, routine manner. Theoretically, every person in the total institution has the same status (in this case, that of criminal), is treated in the same way without any regard for individual differences, and performs almost all activities as part of a group in a forced democracy. On top of that, the prisoner is pretty well cut off from the rest of the world both physically and psychologically. Finally, unlike the person in a school or hospital or monastery, the prisoner is a most unwilling resident of the institution and must be kept under continuing surveillance lest he escape.[4]

Any institution or organization with a strictly ordered routine, which does not allow room for individuality, runs the risk of human rebellion. There is simply a natural contrariness in human beings, which makes us object to being processed in a single groove as though we were a piece of cloth to be properly cleaned in the shortest period of time. Who has not felt the urge to fold, bend, and mutilate that computer card which knows us only as a number? How many children in large groups or in a classroom will act up occasionally just to get personal attention?

Even a factory producing cars or shoes or some *thing* runs a risk. The danger is that the human being who works on the assembly line can become almost like a piece of the machinery, a robot. He becomes bored. No one knows him personally. He is just a time card on a record. The administration knows him only if he slows down production or gums up his machine. He is not personally important. He is a cog in the wheel, a personal nothing.

But the factory is only a limited institution. It does not control all of a man's life. The same man who may be a cog in a wheel all day may be quite a different character when he leaves at night. He may go out at night and show his prowess on the dance floor or at the bowling alley or in the local barroom. He may come home at night and boss his wife or tell the kids how smart he was in school. Or he may dazzle the ladies or drive a powerful car or join a revolutionary movement. He may not be the most delightful person in the world, but he will, in one way or another, express his individual personality. He has friends, lovers, children, and the comforts of even a poor man's life. He is part of a community. In addition, even if his job is a bore, he has the incentive of a paycheck at the end of the week, the hope of rising in the ranks. And, of course, if things are really unbearable, he can always look for a different job. In short, even though his options may be limited, he has some options and he has some outlet in his life-style.

The prisoner has few options. In the first place, he is in the institution twenty-four hours a day. He can't drive a big car; he can't buy fancy clothes; he can't yell at the chef for serving food he doesn't like; he can't even choose his food. He has little or no choice about what kind of work he will do; he can't decide to stay up or out all night; he can't sleep late on Saturday mornings; he can't have a drink with the boys or meet them at the pool room. He can't get into bed with his wife or even dazzle the ladies. He can't peck someone lower on the totem pole, because he is at the bottom. In most prisons, a man (or woman) has no options from which to choose. He has no control over the conduct of his life, over his family, his home, or any of his possessions.

He can't choose anything. And he can do very little about the general physical conditions in which he finds himself. The conditions in prisons vary wildly. The physical plant may be very new, as antiseptic as any operating room; it may have every modern convenience. Each prisoner may have a cell of his own, which he may even be permitted to decorate to his taste.

Or, he may find himself (or herself) in one of our ancient bastions, of which there are too many. There may be two to four people in a cell designed for one or two. There may be rapes on new prisoners, especially the young. There may not even be a toilet in the cell, and he may have to share an ancient, pungent bucket with two or three others. There may be maggots in the food. In short, many prisoners live daily in an atmosphere that would make most of us vomit to see it for only half an hour.[5]

Prisoners also lose all the personal privacy which we normally associate with our human dignity. Few prisons have completely closed doors on the cells. In fact, all too many have only bars through which every corner of the cell is within view of a guard. A prisoner cannot even go to the bathroom in privacy. All prisons have frequent strip-down searches, and when a guard says strip, he means exactly that. Prison administrators regard this as an absolute necessity for keeping weapons and other forms of contraband out of the prison, but there is no question that most prisoners feel the humiliation of these daily searches every time they occur. If other aspects of prison life give one insecure and helpless feelings, they never equal the sense of total defenselessness one feels without even a piece of cloth for protection.

Even a prisoner's thoughts cannot be kept in total privacy, since the practice of censorship still exists in most prisons. Some prisons, including the federal institutions, have voluntarily given up the old practice of censorship. However, as of 1972, only certain aspects of censorship have been declared unconstitutional by the courts. These include the inmate's right to private communications with the courts, counsel, governmental officials, the clergy, and the media. In most prisons, private correspondence with friends and relatives continues to be restricted in terms of the persons to whom inmates may write, the number of letters they may write, and what they may say. The present trend is toward elimination of such practices, but they have by no means been eradicated.[6]

In most instances, a prisoner loses more than the control of his own immediate activities and his pride. Many prisoners lose their homes, their land, and their major possessions because they cannot control their business or personal interests while they are in prison. Most of their families are forced to go on welfare. Worse yet, since criminal conviction in most states is considered a proper ground for divorce, most prisoners lose their spouses. Tragically, they also lose contact with their children and, in some states, their children may even be put up for adoption without their consent.[7]

The continual deprivation of privacy in prison—the strip searches, the censorship of mail, the restrictions on reading materials, restrictions on visitors, restrictions on personal possessions—all are justified by prison administrators under one great blanket theme: *security*.

Security, which includes the prevention of contraband and the prevention of escape, is the primary goal of our prisons. If you doubt the truth of this statement, just look at the budget of any prison. More than 90 percent of all prison budgets is spent on custodial and security costs. Less than 10 percent goes toward education, vocational training, recreation, counseling services, or anything else which would generally come under the heading of "rehabilitation" or "correction." Listening to the rhetoric about corrections is nice, but when you really want to know how a prison (or any organization) functions, you look at the budget. The fact is that anything connected with rehabilitation or correction in prisons is strictly secondary and is permitted only to the degree that it does not interfere with security.

The main reason for the great emphasis on security is that this is really what the public demands of prison officials, and the officials know it quite well. Every member of a prison staff, from the warden down to the newly hired guard on the night shift, knows that security is his first obligation. They all know that, despite all the clamor for prison reform, what most upsets the public is frequent escapes. They know that escapes jeopardize any reform programs they might try. Guards also know that an escape draws the wrath of the district attorney, who wants to let the voters know he is out there protecting public safety, and who will conduct a full investigation into the matter just to prove his dedication to the job. It is a well-known truth that every investigating committee must be able to blame someone.

And every staff member knows that if that someone turns out to be him, he is in a world of trouble.

Thus, every volunteer should remember that the concerns of the staff go in this order: first, security; second, security; third, security. And the more people who move in and out of a prison, the more difficult is the task of maintaining security. Of course, you don't see how you could possibly be any threat, but the suspicious mind can find a threat in many simple-looking acts, looks, movements, or things. Any experienced guard knows that prisoners are a very ingenious group when it comes to finding methods of escape, and what looks harmless to you or me very often doesn't to the security staff.

A man bent on freedom can often think of escape methods which are daring, ingenious, and absolutely creative. One prisoner had a regular visitor who was becoming fairly weary of fulfilling his requests for dental floss, but brought it regularly because he felt dental care was very important and he knew that the prison did not provide floss for inmates. Finally, he no longer had to bring the dental floss because our friendly prisoner had fashioned the abundant supply into a ladder and made his escape the night before his visitor arrived.

Another man observed that even the most highly trained state-police bloodhounds could be distracted by a scent more attractive than that of a prisoner. Thus he made his escape route via the pigpens close to the institution. When the bloodhounds entered the pens, all the pigs went crazy. The dogs decided to chase the pigs and never did catch the escaping prisoner. He had traveled miles and met his prearranged getaway car before the police could even get the dogs out of the pigpen. Having worn out this tactic, another man, much to the delight of the other inmates, had his pickup release a female dog in heat. The damsel successfully detained those fine hounds just long enough to enable the escapee to make a very clean getaway.

Among the many escape stories I've heard, the most ingenious, I thought, was the one in which the prisoners transformed a forklift, which was used daily in the prison industry, into a tank. With it, they plowed right through the gate before the amazed eyes of the guards, whose bullets simply bounced off the homemade armor. This technique, of course, required consider-ably more skill in metalwork than the average prisoner possesses.

At any rate, prisoners spend much of their idle time dream-ing up a never-ending list of escape avenues, and security guards have never-ending nightmares about their possibilities of success. While you and I may entertain wondrous admiration for the cre-ativity of prisoners, you can be quite certain that the prison staff does not. Consequently, you will find that security governs all the actions of the prisoner you may try to help: what he may do, where he may go within the prison, when he may do what, what possessions he may have, what you may or may not give him or do for him, and when and whether you may even see him.

Because of security regulations, every person entering a prison is checked for contraband. The degree of checking will vary from place to place, but particular caution is taken in maximum-security prisons. Most maximum-security prisons will have you pass through a metal detector which will pick up any metallic objects over a certain weight. The idea, of course, is to prevent the entrance of weapons, which cause more worry than any other item on the contraband list. Women are usually asked to leave their purses in a checking station or in a locked box, be-cause so much can be carried through in a large purse. All insti-tutions strictly prohibit alcohol—partly because of tradition and partly because it makes some people vicious. Drugs are prohib-ited, of course, not only because they are illegal, but also because a prisoner on a high may decide to attack an officer. Homemade foods are often prohibited, not so much because the fabled choc-olate cake may contain a hacksaw, but because it may contain LSD or some other drug. The classic and most frequently vio-lated rule is that which forbids the carrying of mail or messages in or out of the prison. I can't think of any sensible reason for limiting a prisoner's mail, but security officials continue to regard mail as a means of making escape plans. Mail censorship is grad-ually breaking down, and may be outlawed by the time this book is printed (though I doubt it), but as of this writing it continues in most prisons across the country.

These are the most common forms of contraband prohib-ited by prisons, but there will be variations on the list from place to place. Some prisons will give you a written list of rules, but in the event that you are not given one, the volunteer should inquire. The best rule of thumb is to declare any item you are bringing into the prison and get permission before you bring it in. Violation of the rules means that you may get the prisoner in trouble if you are caught, and he will suffer for the foolishness of both of you. In all cases, being caught with contraband will result in the volunteer being barred from further entrance to the prison. In some cases, such as the passing of weapons or drugs, the volunteer *and* the prisoner will be subject to prosecution, and the volunteer who was trying to "help" a prisoner could well end up as a prisoner himself.

The stories about contraband and prison escapes are legion, and lots of them are very funny. Some are true and some are pure fantasy. In any event, you may be certain that none of them seems funny to the officials who are in charge when they occur. It is always wise to take prison regulations very seriously. When officials tell you about a rule, they are not joking.

People exposed to such regimentation, total loss of power over their lives, and severe deprivation of all their rights suffer something that, in the long run, may be worse than the physical pains of the old whipping post. They suffer the loss of manhood or womanhood—that most human part of the self, which enables us to have some degree of control, no matter how small, over our own destinies. This loss spells trouble in large letters for the prisoners, the prisons, and for all of us.

There was a classic example of the effect of institutions in the January 1972 issue of *Fortune News*, a monthly publication of a very active organization for penal change, the Fortune Society. The article was entitled "Food in the Prisons" and was written by an understandably unidentified New York State prisoner.

The author said, "Out of all the prison riots over the years, one grievance recurs. That is the demand for better food." He went on to say that the authorities actually purchased food of excellent quality but what the cooks did to it was quite another matter, so that by the time it reached the prisoners' plates, it was nearly inedible. This, he noted, had very serious effects on the bodily functions and on the general health of the men. Near the end of the article, the author proceeded to relate bad food to prison riots once again. He said in his last sentence, "To many recently the question has become a life or death issue. Rahway [New Jersey prison] inmates rioted on the heels of the Attica slaughter—apparently concerned about the consequences, but not concerned enough to be frightened from the act. The question of slow death (by what can be termed 'subtle starvation'), versus quick death from a trooper's shotgun slug, was decided and *they were willing to gamble a quick death against their desire to feel like men*" (italics are mine).

The author of this article has told us more than he may have realized. He has really told us more about institutional life —the total institution—than about his main topic, which was food. Food is the number-one complaint in most prisons, followed by the lack of medical care. After that come guard brutality and the injustice of the system. The complaints are valid more often than one might at first imagine. So, too, are the complaints of officers about working conditions and the attitudes of inmates.

But what would inspire any man, short of the clear and present pangs of starvation, to risk his life because of the quality of food? Prison would.

The food in prison is a problem because it is institutional food. This is not a problem peculiar to prisons. It is common to all institutions which must prepare very large amounts of food, prepare it in advance, and keep it hot until serving-time. I am always amazed, when I see food in a school cafeteria, at the incredible strength of a child's stomach. Just looking at it makes me slightly ill. Many a college boarder, soldier, or sailor can testify to food every bit as bad or worse than that in a prison. And, of course, there is hospital food, which seems so good on the menu. A look at the food tray when it finally arrives will convince any patient that the best way to recover is to get out of the hospital as rapidly as possible. In fact, for some reason which I do not quite understand, the quality of food acquires such an inordinate importance in the lives of almost all people in institutions that it often seems the major topic of conversation.

I don't know what the food was like in the particular institution the writer described. I have little doubt that it was poor by the time he received it. For all we know, it may have been abominable, but I doubt that it was killing anyone. No matter how unappetizing, I don't believe the equally bad food in a school or hospital would drive the average person to violence. But the quality of food in a prison is so important that bad food is sometimes called "riot bait."

The prisoner who wrote the article gave us the most significant clue to the problem in his last sentence. The real issue of which he spoke was not the food, though that was the general topic. The real issue was his desire for manhood. It was not the food that had stripped the prisoner of his sense of manhood; but the food had become a symbol of that loss, just as it does in all prisons. What threatened his sense of manhood was the fact that he was confined in a total institution.

Human beings can survive far greater physical hardships than those suffered by the average American prisoner as a result of poor food or poor medical care. What a human being finds very difficult to survive is the loss of control over his own life and the assault that prison makes on his self-image as a reasonably decent person.

It is this attack on manhood or womanhood—on personhood—that hurts prisoners more than any particular condition they complain about. I say "personhood" because the prisoners' desire to feel like men is not a matter of sexual prowess. It is a matter of their self-image as competent, worthwhile human beings. Self-image is partly "how I see myself" and partly "how the rest of the world sees me," and every human being has to be able to regard himself or herself as a reasonably decent person in order to function properly.

A person who cannot direct even the most simple things in his life, such as what and when to eat or what to read or what to write, is no longer a man or a woman or a full-fledged person. He or she has really only two choices. One is to submit and, over a long period of time, to become the mental infant he is treated as. The person who does this eventually becomes so institutionalized that he can no longer function in the normal world. His mind atrophies like an unused muscle, and he becomes incapable of making the simplest decisions which will be required of him in the world. Such a person will be in trouble again very quickly after he is released from prison.

The second choice is to fight. Some prisoners fight physically either with other prisoners or by rioting against the prison administration. The physical struggle supports their image of themselves as adequate men. Some fight less violently by continually violating minor rules which oppress them—beating the system, so to speak. Others fight psychologically either by withdrawing or by refusing to admit they need anyone's help. They feel they are above such a need, and the feeling of superiority supports their manhood. Or they blame the rest of the world for their condition, because to accept the blame themselves would be too great a threat to their self-image.

The people who fight in any of these ways tend to be unpopular with prison personnel who, quite naturally, prefer cooperation. But the battle they are fighting is often quite necessary to their survival. The battle for survival is great in prison, whether on a physical or psychological level. That's what makes prison such a bad place to be. That's what makes it a scandal.

Some prisoners don't have the strength to survive. Some eventually die the long, slow death of the soul. A few die quickly in riots, because of medical neglect, or by suicide. The latter are relatively few in percentage, but when we consider that prisons are supposed to "rehabilitate," those few must haunt our conscience.

How Bad Are the Bad Guys?

In the spring of 1971 Bacchus Harmon was twenty years old. He had just received a one-and-a-half-year sentence to the county House of Correction for the possession of heroin and a hypodermic needle. It was his first prison sentence.

The county prison, which is considered one of the good ones (if any prison can be called good), did what it could for Bacchus. His withdrawal from heroin was eased by a methadone-withdrawal program. He had a counselor, to whom he would not talk very much. He was encouraged to finish high school while in the prison, and he also took a course in electronics. He joined the group of drug addicts who met regularly to try to help one another. He joined the Fellowship, where he was able to talk with visitors who come each week for discussions with the prisoners. He talked with the chaplain quite a lot. But mostly, he was quiet and withdrawn, and pensively tried to work out his problems without bothering anyone else.

Naturally, there was a limit to what the prison could do for him. It could not cure his drug addiction, which was severe. In fact, it could do very little to help it. It could not change his personal problems, among which was the fact that his parents had been killed when he was eleven years old and his younger brother and sister had disappeared from his sight as wards of another state. It could not relieve his loneliness. Indeed, not until some time later did anyone realize that he never had a personal visitor while he was in prison and never received a letter during the entire nine months he served before he received a parole. No one knew that the forwarding address he gave was a fake that he made up on the spot, and that he really had no relatives, no home, no friends to turn to when he got out of prison. The prison could not help the fact that, although Bacchus was a handsome young black man who was decently educated, he did not have sufficient job skills to acquire a good-paying job. It could not erase the fact that he now carried with him the label of "criminal," though he had never hurt a soul.

Bacchus was out of prison only a few weeks when he was returned to the jail section to await another trial, on two robbery charges. On one occasion Bacchus had tried to rob a marine in order to get money for his heroin. But he wasn't a clever or efficient robber, and the marine was quick and strong. So Bacchus got caught. On the second occasion Bacchus had a gun, which he wasn't tough enough or mean enough to use. He used the gun to hold up a student in Harvard Square, which is a stupid place to try an armed robbery, since it is so crowded. So Bacchus got caught again. Though Bacchus saw himself as a harmless addict, the victim clearly could not agree when faced with a gun. Neither could the police or the judge. Any person who wields a gun has to be considered potentially dangerous.

So now Bacchus sat in jail contemplating two charges of armed robbery (each for a piddling amount of money) and was sure, he felt, to get a fairly stiff sentence to the state prison. He might get twenty years if the judge was hard on addicts or robbers. His future looked pretty grim at that point. A few hours later, he changed it all by hanging himself with his belt.

For six days, his body lay in a morgue while the prison officials tried to locate some friend or relation who would bury him. But Bacchus was to suffer the supreme rejection when, at the age of twenty-one, there was not one soul in the world who would even claim his corpse. Unwanted—alive or dead.

It was only then that we knew that his fellow prisoners in the drug group had been the closest thing to a family that he had. And so, those young men claimed him. The chaplain conducted a funeral service in the prison; the local funeral home donated their services; the florist association sent flowers; the townspeople purchased a grave for him. And the whole prison, both staff and prisoners, mourned not only a little-known brother, but the tragedy of which his life and death were the symbols.

It was a multiple tragedy, beginning with society's indifference to Bacchus's traumatic experience at age eleven, leading to the tragedy of his drug addiction, leading to incarceration, where he learned from others that a "real" robber should have a gun. At last, he became, for the first time, a threat to others.

As is right and just, the death of Bacchus left everyone who knew him—and many who didn't—stunned and shaken. People felt a sense of guilt and responsibility for his tragedy, though the remorse came too late. It made some people begin to contemplate this whole system we call justice and correction. And it forced some to wonder just where the greater guilt should be placed—on Bacchus personally, on the society at large, or on the criminal justice system—and which of these we should most fear.

Was Bacchus in reality so dangerous to society that it was

necessary to lock him in a steel cage for our safety? I don't deny he had committed a crime, but I think he was no worse a man than many who walk with us every day. Many prisoners, though classed permanently as criminals, are no worse than the rest of us, and some are clearly superior to some noncriminals.

Every man, woman, and child in prison is unique just as you and I are. But just as we share enough characteristics so that we can be classified as members of some group, so can the people in prison. Bacchus was a special person whose precise life history will never be duplicated. But there are many ways in which he was similar to the majority of the people you meet when you enter a prison.

First of all, Bacchus was among the small percentage of criminals in this country who are either stupid, inept, or unlucky enough to be caught. The majority are never caught, never mind punished or "rehabilitated." The FBI Uniform Crime Statistics, which are imperfect but the best we have, report on only eight of all possible crimes: murder, negligent manslaughter, forcible rape, and aggravated assault (the four crimes against the person), burglary, larceny, robbery, and auto theft (the four property crimes). And, the FBI can list only the number of crimes reported to the police. It is estimated that there is *at least* three times as much crime as is actually reported, some of this being white-collar crime such as employee theft, some of it serious organized crime and violent crime such as rape.[8]

Of the crimes reported, the ones most frequently solved are murder and manslaughter (there is a body to be accounted for) and aggravated assault and rape (for which there are living witnesses). But these violent crimes represent roughly only 8 percent of all our crimes. Most crimes are thefts and the majority of them go unsolved. Only about one-fourth of all property crimes are solved.[9]

Yet, nearly half (45 percent) of all arrests are for crimes without victims or crimes against public order, such as drunkenness, gambling, liquor law violations, vagrancy, and prostitution. Drunkenness alone accounts for almost one-fourth of all arrests.[10]

Of all those actually arrested, not all are prosecuted. Of those prosecuted, not all are found guilty. And of those found guilty, not all go to prison. Some pay a fine, some get probation. If we compare the millions of crimes reported to the police with the 400,000 or so persons in prison, it is easy to understand why so many prisoners feel they got a bad deal.

It is also simple enough to conclude that they can't all be grisly rapists and murderers. They can't all fulfill the vicious pictures that people conjure up when they imagine what criminals are like. In fact, people serving prison sentences of one year or more are convicted most often on charges of burglary, robbery, larceny, forgery, fraud, and embezzlement.[11] Many of these people, like Bacchus, also happen to be drug addicts who get into stealing to support their habits.

The vast majority of prisoners are, or once were, like Bacchus in that they had their first brush with the law due to a victimless crime. A victimless crime is defined as one based on moral codes in which there is no direct victim except the person who commits the crime. The most common examples of victimless crime are drunkenness, drug addiction, voluntary sexual acts, vagrancy, and gambling. Half of all the people arrested by the police are arrested for victimless crimes, and most of these arrests are for drunkenness. Half of all the people awaiting trial in jail have been charged with victimless crimes, and many of them are convicted and spend a lot of time going in and out of prisons for these crimes. This is known in the trade as doing life on the installment plan.

There is very little any prison can do for a young man or woman whose basic problem is addiction. What the prison can and does do is introduce the minor offender to the genuine criminals who are ready and willing to teach a newcomer the finer tricks of the trade. It can and does expose such a person to a more violent way of life. It does diminish any respect he might have had for the rights of others because it shows him little respect.

It should come as no surprise then that Bacchus graduated from the use of narcotics into the use of a weapon for armed robbery. Whether he was effective in using the weapon is another matter entirely. He learned where and how to get it, which is not difficult in a country which refuses to outlaw handguns.

Many offenders who started out the way Bacchus did actually become dangerous as a result of what they learn in prison. One study done in Pennsylvania focused on a group of men who had been released from prison and were returned to the prison for a new crime. Thirteen of the men had originally been convicted in cases which involved weapons. One hundred and one men were returned to prison (on parole violation) for carrying weapons. The same pattern continued in a whole list of other crimes: "18 of them had been originally committed as drug and narcotic offenders, whereas eleven of the eighteen were returned to prison for new drug crimes—plus 103 other parolees returned for drug offenses. . . . 13 parolees had been originally convicted for carrying weapons—but 101 of those returned were returned for this crime." [12] The same pattern held true in the study of 3,424 parolees. It was the same pattern followed by Bacchus.

Of course, it would be clearly dishonest to give the impression that all the people in prison are harmless souls who simply happen to have a vice of which society disapproves. Not all are quiet and gentle like Bacchus. Not all are decent people. A few are violent and brilliant, some are violent and illiterate, and others are just plain violent and rotten to the core by the time the prison gets them.

Most of those convicted of a victimless crime are found in the county prisons because most of these crimes are misdemeanors. What constitutes a misdemeanor can vary somewhat from place to place, but it is always considered a less serious crime, and usually carries a prison sentence of no more than two and a half years.

Those who are convicted of a felony, that is, a more serious crime, generally receive a longer sentence and are sent to one of the larger, more secure state prisons or penitentiaries. However, even in these large prisons, you will find only a small percentage of prisoners who have committed the more sensational crimes such as murder and rape, the kind of crimes that really scare most people. Even there the majority of the prisoners are serving time for property crimes.

But, just because they haven't committed murder does not mean they are all nice guys. An inmate of Attica prison in New

York said in a letter to the *New York Times,* "Many convicts are criminal scum whose sole purpose in life closely parallels that of a demented crocodile. They wouldn't lead an honest life if guaranteed a thousand dollars per week and half of God's throne in the hereafter." Another ex-inmate of the Massachusetts state prison at Walpole agreed, saying, "The worst part of being in prison is the forced democracy, the forced mixing with guys you wouldn't spit on outside the walls. . . . If a guy was scum on the street, chances are high that he'd be scum inside."

But even he agreed that what he called the "criminal scum" only amounted to about 5 percent of the prison population. The vast majority are more like the author of the letter, who seemed to regard himself as a fairly decent fellow.

Many prisoners are similar to Bacchus in yet more ways. He was poor, and he was black. A young, white, middle-class, well-dressed offender who was polite to the police most likely would never have gone to prison for the first narcotics offense, or even for the second. You have probably read, as I have, of the children of nationally known people who received only a reprimand from the judge for a similar offense. Their parents came for them immediately, they hired the very best lawyers, agreed to supervise the youth, and the matter was virtually ended. But, like many of those who are either poor or black, or both, Bacchus had no one to stand by him or vouch for him. He could hope for nothing more than a public defender who wouldn't have time to spend on his case and who would generally advise, "Plead guilty and I think I can get you a short sentence." So he would be punished where the more affluent would not be punished—at least not with prison. And his punishment would go with him through life as a criminal record. It has always been that the poor have paid for their sins in this life, and, generally (though not always) the rich have been able to postpone their debt until the next.

Lastly, like a lot of other prisoners, Bacchus was a school dropout, and he lacked readily marketable skills. He didn't have a home, he was rootless and drifting around trying to find himself a place in a world that didn't give a damn about him or what he did or where he went, so long as he didn't give anyone any bother. Most of the time he was no bother. Even the prison guards said that. No bother at all. Just a quiet, desperate, inadequate young man about whom nobody cared until he committed a great act of violence: suicide.

Whether the person in prison is disturbed like Bacchus or is more like a "demented crocodile," he suffers the same effects. All prisoners find that prison life has detrimental effects on their personalities, on their future associations, and on their entire lives. Whatever they were like before they came to prison, the chances are very high that one of the effects of prison will be to lead them to more problems and more crime, rather than less.

Some prisoners, who are fairly capable people who happened to get caught, don't need your help at all. The only thing you can do for them is to help break up the routine boredom of prison life, help them to maintain contact with the outside, and help maintain their self-respect until they reach the day of release.

Many others in prison desperately need concrete help, whether or not they admit it. They may need whatever help can be had for their addiction to alcohol or narcotics. They may need education or job training or encouragement in legitimate use of leisure time. Some of them may need human friendship and support, or all of these things combined. After long prison terms, many may need help in finding a home or a job or in adjusting to ordinary life.

No honest person who has any association with prisons would suggest that prison is a good place in which to provide the services which so many of our offenders need. Many of our prisons could be emptied out, the money and personnel used to provide special services in the community, and the offenders and the community would be much better off.

However, only the utopian dreamer can believe that prisons are going out of style in the near future. Ask yourself how many prisons have closed in the last year or two. Instead of being closed up, new prisons are being built. There is a powerful social resistance to closing or changing institutions which people imagine add to their safety. Of course, for the most part it is quite an imaginary or, at best, very short-lived safety. But, so long as people believe in this safety, they will resist changes.

Therefore, prisons will be with us for longer than I care to contemplate. Even as we may take small steps toward utopia, we will always have a few people who are truly dangerous to our safety and who cannot be left free.

So long as we have any prisons, and we have thousands in operation today, we need many, many volunteers to help reduce the evil effects of prison life. We need people who don't know about all the "things that can't be done," people who have the imagination and the grit to change what can be changed, to close many prisons, and to find new ways of working with those offenders—the majority—who are not a danger to the community.

No institution is likely to change itself. Employees don't rock the boat, and prisoners are almost powerless to cause orderly change. Justice is too important to be left only to professionals—the community must help. Since the prisons can't come to the community, the community—the volunteers—must go to the prison.

Seldin Jones was a thief, and not the smartest one around, it was clear, because he was caught on several occasions. The first time, he faced the judge with tears in his big blue eyes, promised to return to his mother, and said he would never steal again. The second time around, he faced the judge with more tears, and because he was young and the local jail was a bad place and he had been caught with only one wallet, which was returned to the owner, he was placed on probation. The third time, he wept copiously as he was dragged off for a short term in the local hoosegow. The fourth time, he faced an angry judge who said, "By golly, you're going to learn a lesson." He drew three to five years in the state prison.

Well, it was soon learned that Seldin was very much handicapped by a lack of education. What sort of decent job can you get with an eighth-grade education? Some sort of unskilled labor, it's true, but Seldin had a champagne taste and couldn't seem to get by with the small pay to be gleaned from such jobs. The prison didn't have much to offer, but it did have a school. Thus, once he had overcome the shock of being in prison, Seldin settled into school to study his way out. It was commendable, the staff thought, and Seldin worked hard, passing the high school equivalency test in three years. Not so dumb, after all.

Parole came easily as the board reviewed his clean record and accomplishments, and heard him explain that he now felt well equipped for a new life. So

2

KEYS TO CHANGE: VOLUNTEER PROGRAMS

off he went, got a job, and returned to his home. Not a year had passed before the parole officer realized that a significant change had taken place in Seldin. No longer was he an uneducated thief. He was now a high-school-graduate thief, confidently stealing almost twice the amount he had managed in the teary-eyed days. His champagne taste had not changed, of course, and neither had his destination: another term in the state prison.

I tell you about Seldin mainly to illustrate a problem which exists in programs in prison, whether they are staff-operated or volunteer-run. What do you do with a young man like Seldin? How do you change his behavior or his attitudes enough so that he ceases to be a continuing nuisance to the community? The problem is that, for all the theorizing that goes on, nobody knows exactly what means, which programs, or which persons can create the spark in Seldin which might induce him to stay within the law.

Studies have been done comparing groups of offenders who go to prison with groups of offenders who are put on probation. It has been found that a certain percentage of those in each group will be multiple repeaters of crime whether they receive the harshness of prison or the comparatively easier penalty of probation.[1] A few will grow into dangerous men. The difficulty is that, if some 20 to 30 percent are repeaters, no one can tell in advance precisely which 20 to 30 percent will be the repeaters.

The same logic and the same problem apply to programs in prisons. We know that educational programs will help a certain percentage of prisoners to stay away from crime in the future, but we are never sure about which persons will be affected. Nor do we know just how effective an education can be in preventing future crime. We know that job training and placement will have a salutary effect on some prisoners, but we never know for sure on which ones or on exactly how many.

Seldin is not a statistic. He is a person—a round peg—who did not fit into any square statistic about what ought to happen. Perhaps, although I don't know for sure, Seldin simply enjoys the continuing challenge of being a thief—the challenge of the hustle—and no amount of schooling or job training is going to provide him with the same thrill. He courts disaster and likes the sensation of missing it by a hairsbreadth. He has something of the gambler's instinct, which is quite difficult to exercise in a legitimate fashion.

While professionals in the field of corrections worry about men like Seldin—in fact, worry a great deal—they are forced by the sheer weight of numbers and budgetary limits to gear their programs to the majority. This is because, as we have seen briefly, institutions are supposed to operate on the principle of efficiency. That is, institutions are designed to process the maximum number of persons while employing the least number of personnel. A few people must serve and/or control many. In most instances, what is supposed to be service quickly degenerates into simple control and security. The problem is that the ability to control people via weapons or locks and bars has no connection whatsoever with changing them.

When we want to change people and help them grow and mature and accept responsibility, we use a principle exactly the opposite of efficiency. One administrator I met calls it the principle of redundancy. This is the same principle we use in ordinary life. A child is exposed to many kinds of personalities before he is fully developed. He sees people functioning in a variety of careers before he chooses one of his own. He dates many people before deciding on a spouse. He mulls over many ideas before finally developing a life-style of his own. If an individual at mid-life changes any important aspect of his life, such as his career or spouse or religion, he examines many new possibilities before making a choice so that he can make the best possible choice for himself.

But in ordinary life we are in a community where we can make the necessary contacts with a wide variety of persons and ideas. The prisoner is in a system which is specifically designed to limit his contacts. Ideally, the prisoner should also be in the community, even if under supervision. However, the reality is that he is not and many prisoners will not be for a very long time. Therefore, until such time as we advance to genuine community corrections, the major alternative is to bring the principle of redundancy into the prison.

Under this principle, we would provide many persons—both

paid personnel and unpaid volunteers—for each offender in custody. No one knows exactly what, who, when, or how human behavior can be influenced or changed. The prisoner who cannot relate to me because I'm too middle-class may relate very well to a white-haired old man who uses the prisoner's slang and represents the father figure he has unknowingly sought. One man's life may be changed by the books he finds in a good library. Another may be touched by the basketball star who visits the prison and explains his techniques. A discussion group may open one man's soul; music may reach another. One man finds a vocation in repairing motorcycles; another in architecture. Another needs no vocational training, but needs to find a legitimate, interesting recreation to keep him out of barroom brawls. And the last may be like Seldin. He may have to be exposed to many people and ideas and activities before anything will make a difference. Because each person's background, abilities, experiences, likes, and dislikes are different, there is no *one* kind of program, activity, or person that can have an effect on all prisoners.

The ideal program in a prison, then, tries to bring all this—the community itself—into the prison. The office of the director of volunteers ought to function as a channel for screening and training volunteers, for helping to place them in any one of a variety of activities, and for helping volunteers, staff, and inmates to develop new opportunities. A good program requires the use of imagination—quite contrary to the "this is the way we always did it" pattern in most places. It demands the suspension of theories that say if a program doesn't work with the majority, it is useless. It demands a belief that, though human behavior may not be perfectible, it can change, for the hope of change is the hope of the world.

I regret to say, however, that such a broad and open program, based on the principle of redundancy, is not what you are likely to find in the average prison. You may find only one of the programs described below, or you may find nothing at all. If you find nothing, or if the volunteer program needs to be broadened, you can get more information on model programs by writing to the organizations listed in the back of this book.

Like everything else in prisons, volunteer programs are generally designed to fit the needs of the majority. Those programs which appear to make advances in reducing recidivism and, at the same time, do not interfere with the security and internal order of the prison, are the ones which are most common and best accepted by prison administrators. They are limited in variety both for you, the volunteer, and for the prisoner; therefore, their usefulness is also limited. But in spite of their limitations, many of them are excellent programs, and there are several broad types into which you may be welcomed.

A Variety of Model Programs

Among the programs you are most likely to find are those which attempt to produce an internal change in the offender by helping him recognize his responsibility for his acts. Having done this, the programs then try to give the offender the support he needs to effect a change in his behavior. There are several different techniques used in these programs.

The Fellowship model, such as the one at the Massachusetts Correctional Institution at Norfolk, can be found in a number of prisons across the country. Volunteer citizens engage in regular discussion groups with those prisoners who wish to join the Fellowship. Through this interaction, it is hoped the offender will examine some of the attitudes that got him into trouble in the first place and will feel the support and concern of the community for him. Also, it is hoped that the volunteer will act as a resource and helping hand to the inmate when he is released so he may avoid future criminal acts. Many ex-convicts who never could have made it alone are now living fruitful lives as a result of this Fellowship program.

Among the variations on this basic theme is a program that trains and engages citizens in group counseling of prisoners. The program at the Bucks County Jail, Pennsylvania, called Imaginal Education, is an example of this technique. It is based on the theory that criminal behavior is largely a result of poor self-image, which leads the offender to believe he is the victim of circumstances, rather than the creator of them. Because he sees himself as a victim, he cannot take responsibility for his decisions. For example, the armed robber who kills a policeman may say, "But he saw that I had a gun on him, and still he reached for his. Did he think I was going to stand there and get killed? It was me or him. He shouldn't have reached for his gun. It was his own fault."

Imaginal Education counseling helps the offender see life as a series of situations or circumstances with many possibilities. He must make the decision about how a situation will proceed. He is responsible. He had a gun and was perpetrating a robbery; he set up the situation so that a death could easily occur. Volunteers are trained to develop and teach the tools of decision-making. Not only does this assist individuals in accepting responsibility for their acts, but it helps them set goals for their lives. They see how one goes about setting a long-range goal and then making a series of decisions that will help them arrive at that goal.

This program is effective with many offenders because it zeroes in on what is actually their basic problem. It is now incorporated under the name Thresholds, and is gradually spreading to other institutions. Both this and the Fellowship model involve group actions.

Another form of social attention is the formation of one-to-one relationships between volunteers and offenders. Such programs are based on the knowledge that many offenders have never known anyone who really cared about them. They have had no one to trust, no one to provide a model. The process of trying to pull together a decent life alone is simply too overwhelming, especially for those who have had little decency extended to them. The one-to-one relationship begins while the offender is still in prison, and he or she, always on a voluntary basis, is matched to an outside volunteer with similar interests in life.

One very successful program of this kind has been the Man-to-Man (M-2) Sponsors in the state of Washington, and similar projects have spread to California and other Western states. In Minnesota, a program almost identical to M-2 operates under the name Amicus. And in North Carolina, it is simply called Community Volunteers. The North Carolina Department of Corrections has taken the one-to-one-relationship idea a step further and permits the honor-grade inmate to leave the prison in the company of his volunteer friend to participate in cultural, educational, sports, or other legitimate interests they have in common.

In each program, the purpose of the volunteer friend is to offer needed personal and moral support while the offender is still in prison, to be a source of knowledge of community resources, to be a helper in locating a job, and to be a firm source of aid in the difficult task of reentering a hostile and wary community. In Washington State, the M-2 program is one phase of Job Therapy, Inc., a clear indication that all friendship, assistance, and mutual pleasure are geared toward successful functioning at the time of release. In short, even the pleasures have a most serious purpose.

So difficult is the task of finding acceptance in the community and adjusting to noninstitutional life, especially following a long period of confinement, that several programs gear all their volunteer effort to pre-release preparation.

The state of Texas has a pre-release program on which many others are modeled. Inmates who are within four to six weeks of completing their prison sentence are sent to a pre-release center, and here the security regulations are relaxed. Inmates enter the wider community for certain activities and receive an intensive five-week course covering areas of life which are known to present the biggest problems for them: employment, law, finances, family problems, and the general community. Volunteers who have special knowledge of these problems participate in the courses as guest speakers, and others are paid speakers. Still others join in the recreational programs of the center, assist through an organization such as the Jaycees, or help by employing ex-inmates. Though the nature of the center limits the volunteers participating mostly to professionals, this limited group performs very important work.

Another type of pre-release guidance is given by successful ex-inmates who volunteer to help those just about to come out of prison. Their contribution, though limited by law or custom

in many parts of the country, is very important. Most prison inmates meet only the failures who are returned to prison either
for parole violation or a new crime. The volunteer ex-inmates
not only provide a living model of success, but have been
through exactly the same problems the releasees are about to
face. They know how it feels and how difficult the task is, but
they also know it can be done. Ex-inmates have a degree of
credibility among many prisoners that the rest of us, no matter
how good our intentions, will never have.

While you may not be able to participate directly in such a
program (if you have never been incarcerated), you may be
among the many citizens who can support the program indirectly. The projects using volunteer ex-inmates have two prongs:
pre-release guidance and direct assistance upon release in finding
a home, a job, or whatever the newly released prisoner needs.
Pre-release guidance may involve a combined effort of ex-
inmates, volunteers, and paid personnel. Ex-inmates may continue their support when a prisoner is released, but it is asking a
great deal to expect the usually small groups of ex-inmates to locate temporary housing, jobs, training, and counseling that the
newly released person needs. Volunteer help is needed for these
tasks.

The Fortune Society (which operates chiefly in New York
and New Jersey), the Seventh Step (which began at the Kansas
State Penitentiary and spread to the West), and Project Re-
Entry at the Correctional Institution at Norfolk, Massachusetts,
are only a few examples of programs in which ex-inmates and
volunteer citizens work together. This is a growing movement,
and there are many small groups of ex-inmates developing all
across the country. But they cannot function adequately without
community support. They have a valid role to play in helping
prisoners and ex-prisoners and should be encouraged.

The last variation of the social-problem-centered program is
the self-help type. At least one of these can be found in almost
every prison—even those prisons which generally discourage volunteers. Of the most commonly found self-help groups, Alcoholics Anonymous undoubtedly has the oldest record of acceptance
in prisons. Drug groups, which operate under a wide variety of

names, have evolved more recently and are increasingly necessary, since the number of drug addicts continues to rise in prisons. Finally, in some prisons you will find Gamblers Anonymous, although it has a smaller following than the other two groups. Each of these programs depends in some measure for its resources on the assistance of volunteers who are not alcoholics, drug addicts, or gamblers. Sometimes moral support is needed, sometimes financial help. And volunteers also help administer the organizations.

Education and Job Training

The second broad category of volunteer involvement overlaps in some ways with social-attention programs, but it is useful to make a distinction here. Since most prison inmates have not completed high school and many have not finished elementary school, and since educational deficiency is a clear handicap on the job market, it is fairly obvious that educational facilities are vitally important in prison. While education by itself is no cure for crime—as no single program is—it is extremely valuable to most prisoners in increasing their options in life.

However, the President's Crime Commission Report, published in 1967, found that most educational programs are concentrated only in the large prisons and penitentiaries. Very few programs exist in the more than 4,000 county institutions. The report stated that the national ratio of academic teachers to prisoners was one teacher for every 1,333 prison inmates. This ratio may have improved a little since 1967, but I wager that the improvement has been very small. Considering the magnitude of the educational needs, such a ratio is scandalous. This is an area in which there is the greatest need for volunteers. Part of the educational task can and is being done in some places by volunteer college students. However, there is ample room for other citizens who have a decent education and a few hours a week to spare.

Specifically, volunteers are needed who can provide individual tutoring for illiterate prisoners, of whom there are quite a few. And people who can give courses in high school subjects, especially mathematics and English, to prepare inmates for high school equivalency tests are also needed.

Even in those institutions which have educational programs, the few teachers available are generally swamped with more students than they can possibly handle, and the result is often robotlike courses. There is a need for imaginative people who can transmit subject matter without the sense of grinding drudgery which so often created a school dropout to begin with.

To a lesser extent, but important nevertheless, is the need for college-level courses. Currently, most college-level courses are available to inmates only on a correspondence basis, the least desirable and most discouraging method known of acquiring an education.

Conveniently for volunteers, teachers of all varieties are most needed in small county institutions which house misdemeanants serving short sentences. These are the institutions which are likely to be nearest your home. Their need is for courses designed to be taught over a short period of time. Exactly this kind of program, almost totally dependent on citizen participation, was developed for the Westchester County Penitentiary in New York.

In 1962, the Westchester Citizens Committee began a four-month experiment in teaching illiterate and semi-illiterate inmates to read. A special teacher was paid by an anonymous citizen, and the classes were held five nights of the week, two hours for each session. In three months, several men had increased their reading levels by one to three grades. It wasn't long before the program was expanded to include mathematics, and eventually to include studies toward a high school equivalency diploma. The courses are short and intensive and are successful. They have persisted over the years, in spite of funding problems which several times caused a temporary suspension of the program.

Vocational or career training that is of any significance for the majority of prisoners may be in even shorter supply than academic training. There are two main reasons for this. The first is that most states limit prison industry to materials produced for the state itself (for example, license plates) so that such industry will not compete with private enterprise.

Secondly, when training a prisoner for a career he can pursue upon release, one must automatically eliminate all jobs which are closed to him only because he has a criminal record. This includes virtually all the professions, civil service jobs, and public offices. I know that history records a few classic exceptions to this prohibition (such as James Michael Curley of Boston, who was elected mayor while in prison), but such instances are classic precisely because they are so exceptional. The prohibition on jobs for ex-inmates also usually includes almost all work for which a license is required or for which a worker must be bonded; work that requires a security clearance (such as defense industries); and employment that involves trust or the handling of money. And there are thousands of jobs closed to ex-inmates simply because people generally distrust anyone who has even once committed a crime, and just won't hire him. All in all, about half the jobs in this country are closed to ex-inmates either by law or by custom, so there is no sense in training inmates in these vocations.

Yet, we know that successful employment is a most crucial factor in preventing a return to crime. The prejudicial atmosphere which now exists will change only as more employers become involved with the problems of prisoners. Though prejudice is disappearing at an agonizingly slow pace, it is beginning to decrease through a number of programs like the following:

Job Therapy, Inc. in Washington state, includes a job bank in its program, as well as Man-to-Man Sponsors, which I mentioned earlier. Job Therapy canvasses industries, professions, and all types of employers and conducts a Job Success Institute, which surveys opportunities and requirements for jobs. It also assists in the actual job search and gives job guidance and training in sheltered workshops, as well as running a pre-release center.

Pace Institute at the Cook County Jail in Chicago functions on the same theory, but works exclusively with short-term prisoners. Pace begins by establishing literacy or high school education, and then offers beginning trade training while a man is inside the institution. Advanced training is provided through schools and workshops outside the prison. Job opportunities are also sought for the men, and the job path is cleared by advocates, where otherwise it would have been difficult or impossible.

In some instances, individual companies, directed by people of social conscience, act as volunteers. One example of this is the Honeywell Corporation. They lent their employees to the prison, and also provided the equipment, to set up a computer training center in the Massachusetts Correctional Institution at Walpole. Certain inmates were trained to train others, while the company continued supervision of the program and helped place trainees in jobs upon release.

Other companies, such as Polaroid, while not creating a training center, permit employees to take a leave of absence so they can put their talents and training to work in a social-problem area such as a prison.

Through the efforts of dedicated directors or other employees, more companies are beginning to hire ex-inmates for the first time. The door is beginning to open, but only by a tiny crack. More industries and businesses could and should become involved in tapping this very large source of manpower.

One organization which has worked most diligently on a nationwide scale to place releasees in jobs is the United States Jaycees. A Jaycee chapter can be found in at least one prison (and often in more than one) in every state of the nation. And a network of local chapters aids in placing ex-inmates in jobs wherever their homes may be located. While they don't generally engage in job training inside the prison, they do help provide the end product, a job, without which all possible training is quite useless.

The third common type of volunteer assistance that is desperately needed is legal counsel. Most prisoners have limited economic means or none at all. They cannot afford a defense lawyer, and they receive only minimal assistance from the vastly overburdened public defenders, who are paid by the state to defend the indigent. By and large, members of the legal profession have not leaped at the opportunity to counsel on a voluntary basis. However, there has been a continuing and growing interest among law students to do so. More than seventy-five law schools now have organizations similar to Harvard's Voluntary Defenders. Through this program, senior law students are permitted to defend indigent clients in court and/or assist a public defender in gathering evidence for a case. However, many courts and prisons are not adjacent to a large law school, and many law schools do not have programs of this type. The participation of experienced lawyers is needed.

The last broad group of programs in which volunteers can and very often do participate are leisure-time activities. These activities are more significant than many people think, for several reasons. First of all, time is the one thing that there is plenty of in a prison. Time hangs heavy and passes slowly for anyone who is incarcerated. And lack of something to do can produce trouble inside a prison far more quickly than in the outside world, where there are at least more attractions and distractions. Secondly, most prisoners are young men who need ways of working off the physical and psychic energy they naturally accumulate. Finally, many inmates have never learned how to put spare time to constructive and enjoyable use, and many youths who are in prison today might not have committed illegal acts if they had had something better to do. Some of them develop an intense interest in sports, hobbies, or arts, which they never had a chance to develop previously and which just might help them keep out of trouble in the future. And for a few prisoners, activities which begin as pleasant pastimes grow into vocations or professions.

Almost all, but not all, large prisons have some sports facilities for inmates. The most commonly found will be at least a basketball hoop, if not a gym or standard basketball court. Most large prisons also have a field that can be used for baseball or football. The greatest lack of sports facilities exists in small county institutions, which are often hampered by a lack of funds, and in overcrowded jails where there is literally no physical space in which to put any kind of facility.

There are several ways volunteers can assist in sports. First, make sure the prison has some sports activity, and if it doesn't, try to start something. Even in jails where the only exercise space is the corridor immediately in front of the cells, a movable basketball hoop can be placed at one end.

If the prison has facilities, make sure they are being used. For example, a gym which is proudly displayed to visitors touring the prison is utterly useless if the inmates are not permitted to go into it or if the equipment is always locked up. If a prison has a shortage of officers to supervise a facility such as a gym, you'll find that athletic activities are simply canceled. This situation can be relieved by a group of volunteers who can be present to supervise and join in the sports, or teach the inmates various sports when there is no staff to do so.

There may already be a good sports program inside the institution. Many prison softball and basketball teams are excellent. But there is nothing that will raise the spirit and effort of a team like the challenge of meeting an outside team. I have seen local high school and college championship basketball teams absolutely trounced by inmate teams. The inmates had practiced for weeks, of course, almost to the point of exhaustion, in preparation for the games. Groups such as the lawyers softball league are, naturally, a cinch to defeat.

The most fiercely competitive game one can witness occurs in the institution where I volunteer: the Inmates vs. Officers basketball game. One can always predict the date of the event because food consumption decreases in the officers' dining room as everyone gets into shape, and inmates stream to the gym to work out. The outcome is equally predictable: the inmates always win. The one absolute necessity in a game of this kind is an ample supply of very strong volunteer referees.

Volunteers can also be instrumental in developing a wider variety of sports activities. Not everyone likes to play basketball or baseball, though they may observe them with pleasure. Furthermore, these sports require a whole team, which the prisoner may not easily find after his release. It is more desirable to encourage an interest in those sports that an inmate can pursue with either one or two people, or alone, and in an institution that has a gym it can be done easily.

With the increase in movable sporting equipment, it is no great feat to put a gym to multiple use. One gym can provide the setting for the following sports: basketball, indoor track, street hockey, tennis, Ping-Pong, boxing, wrestling, and weight-lifting. I would love to see a prison in which such a variety of sports exists, but I haven't seen one yet.

It is unfortunate that in most prisons art, music, drama,

dance, creative writing, and handicrafts are considered to be either harmless time-fillers or luxuries prisoners don't need. I don't sense any objection to the arts in prisons, just indifference. As a result, pursuit of the arts is generally neglected or nonexistent, unless there is a volunteer corps to encourage it or unless the inmates undertake it on their own. Yet, the arts can be excellent leisure-time activities for prisoners, and can be potential vocations for gifted inmates. Although the artistically gifted are a minority in prisons, just as they are outside, they should not be overlooked.

Volunteers do assist in the arts in many institutions, and they generally receive an encouraging response from the prisoners. The response from staff is often cool, especially if the volunteer artist sports long hair or a beard, but even the offbeat are becoming more acceptable.

An example of possible involvement is in the visual arts. Prisoner art and public displays of it are more and more frequently seen. Many individual artists offer their time to give instruction to small classes in the techniques of various media, including photography, even though there are limitations and problems in prisons the artists are not accustomed to on the outside. One inmate-artist complained that he could not work on a landscape because all he could see was the cellblock. The guard said, "That's tough," and that was the end of the landscape. Another inmate was quite gifted, and a volunteer obtained a commission for him to prepare silk-screen signs for a convention in Boston. However, the prison-made signs were so nice they were promptly stolen by the "good" people on the outside. I suppose this is known as poetic justice.

Groups of people also try to foster prisoner art. Under the auspices of the Stone Foundation in Chicago, a group of volunteers opened and now runs a store in the city in which prisoner art is displayed and sold, and proceeds go to the artists. The Floating Foundation of Photography in New York conducted a photographic workshop at a New York prison and took on the responsibility of displaying the results for the general public.

However, most prison artwork is sold only in the shops found at prison gates, where few of the public come and few works are sold. Thus, few inmates are encouraged to continue their work. Greater volunteer participation is needed both in teaching art and in providing adequate outlets for it.

Music is the language common to us all, loved in one form or another by everyone, and prisoners are no exception. A few prisons have their own bands and even band leaders, and some have chapel choirs. However, in most prisons, the only instrument available is a radio. There is little or no opportunity for active participation in music.

In a few places, such as Jessup, Maryland, a group of volunteers who are professional musicians have teamed up with inmates to form musical groups that perform regularly. The Jessup group, called Sound, presents biweekly performances of rock music for the inmate population.

In Massachusetts, the New England Conservatory of Music, via a special grant, sends music teachers to the Middlesex County House of Correction, in a program similar to those in which industry offers its personnel to prisons. The professional teachers are paid, but as far as the prison and inmates are concerned, the contribution is voluntary, since an outside group directs the program and assumes the cost. This particular program is conducted not only to give the prisoners enjoyment, but also to offer instruments and instruction to those who wish to study music as a possible career.

And, of course, famous professional musicians perform from time to time in prisons without charge. There are many unknown, but able, performers who could also participate in prison programs if there were more people to make contacts and bring them to the prisons.

Creative writing, for the most part, is pursued by inmates entirely on their own, and much of the fiction, articles, and poetry which pours out of prisons indicates a clear lack of training. A gifted poet or journalist, like an artist or musician, has a talent that cannot be taught; it just is. However, even gifted writers need training in mastering various techniques, and journalists, poets, or free-lance writers can offer this training. Considering the near absence of training, it is amazing that so much good writing has come out of prisons. A fairly sizable list of famous writers is included in the ranks of those who have produced works from a prison cell.

Theatrical art is woefully neglected in most prisons, but may be spreading because of two good programs. Theatre for the Forgotten in New York City presents dramas inside the prison and also trains inmates as actors or members of the stage crew, and the Elma Lewis School of Fine Arts in Roxbury, Massachusetts, provides a similar program at the Massachusetts Correctional Institution in Norfolk.

Crafts of some sort are pursued in many prisons, but not to the extent they might be if more volunteers would assist. Very often, certain crafts, such as leather-tooling, are pursued as small businesses and the products are sold in prison stores with the inmates getting the profits.

However, the types of crafts available are limited because of the lack of materials, equipment, or someone to teach the craft. Also, the market in prison stores is very limited. The marketing possibilities can grow where they are not limited by law, but they need volunteers. Prisoners can operate a store at the prison gate, but they can't run one in the downtown section of a city. They may be able to make things with leather or wool or other materials, but they can't go out to shop for these materials.

This sounds like a fairly extensive list of volunteer programs, and one might be tempted to question the need for more volunteers. However, those I have listed are model programs which do not yet exist in most prisons. You may find a rare institution which offers every activity on my list, but usually you'll find that most prisons have either one or two activities modeled on one of the programs listed above, or, they have nothing at all.

If a prison has no programs at all, the problem is too obvious to require discussion. If it offers one or two activities, every inmate is expected to accept them cheerfully and with gratitude. But, by what strange manner of thinking can anyone presume that all prison inmates have the same tastes or talents, any more than the rest of us do? What rational basis can be found for the assumption that one fellowship or basketball team or course in art or job as a sheet-metal worker is going to appeal to every prisoner?

The usual response to these questions is, "Those bums should be grateful for whatever they get. No one took away their rights. They forfeited them, and I don't care whether they like it or not." It's quite true that they forfeited their freedom as a result of their acts, but it is not true that we should not care about their needs. We should care if for no other reason than that the problems we do not help prisoners solve while they are in prison will come back to us and our communities when they are released. And we must keep in mind that 97 percent of all prisoners are released at some point. They are coming back to us a few at a time, every day of the year. Therefore, we had better care.

Perhaps, just perhaps, if Seldin had found a pursuit which was challenging or reasonably profitable, in addition to his education, he might have gone straight. I would hate to be put in the position of trying to prove that any given activity or person could change Seldin's ways, but it's important to note that no one can prove the contrary either. In dealing with human behavior, there are simply very few proofs for anything.

We know that the majority of offenders can benefit from programs, whether the activities are inside or outside a prison. But our greatest problems are not with the majority. They are with the minority of prisoners, the Seldins, who cannot be reached with traditional means. One man like Seldin can account for a great many crimes. And he will continue in a pattern of crime unless someone makes an effort to break the cycle.

A sense of reality compels me to add that there will probably always be a small percentage of offenders who will never fit into law-abiding patterns of life, just as there will always be a small percentage of people in any society who are physically, mentally, emotionally, or socially unable to abide by the majority's standards. Society's task is not to eliminate crime, but to keep the criminal percentage down to the lowest level possible so that the majority may live in peace. The efforts we have made toward this end in prisons are far from satisfactory.

Let us now consider whether—and how—you could fit into one of the models described, or how you might branch out into something entirely new.

Ellen stopped halfway up the prison stairs to the dining hall, where a Fellowship meeting was to take place. It was her weight that made her gasp. Just short of obesity, she had the copious flesh of middle age which makes it quite impossible to tell where the hips end and the breasts begin or whether certain angles are caused by a fold of fat or the stay of a corset. But above all the convolutions of her body emerged a happy, pretty, naïve, smiling face. It was the face of an imperturbable optimist who could make even an undertaker smile.

3

THE OBSTACLE COURSE FOR VOLUNTEERS

Ellen was one of the volunteers who came regularly for the weekly discussion groups of the Fellowship. She surprised me a little the first time I saw her. She was surrounded by a group of young convicts, all in their early twenties. They were the same fellows who talk sex all the time and who would readily kneel in adoration of the *Playboy* centerfold. Since I saw no relation between Ellen and the centerfold, I had no comprehension of why the men seemed to regard her as the most honored guest.

I soon discovered the reason for their attraction to her. Ellen was not only a warm human being, but she was a great listener. Her ears were constantly ready to hear what people said, to catch the nuances of meanings, of prisoners' problems, in order to know how she could help. She did this because she cared about them, not because of what they could give her or because of who they were, but because she was interested in them as human beings. Her attractiveness was that she had a gift for making each one of these young men feel like a very important person.

And because she cared, she always remembered what they had discussed the week before, recalling the details of each one's problems. There were some things she couldn't do much about, but her concern helped to make the problems a little more bearable. "Is your wife a little better this week?" and she would hear the details about his wife's progress, and remember them. "Was the English exam as bad as you expected?" and out would pour all his feelings about the exam and his pride at having passed. She would share his joy.

She remembered the things that she could do something about. She got permission to bring in a can of paint which was to become a mural on one man's wall. In her pocket was another man's favorite cigar. And out of the mysterious depths of yet another pocket came the hometown paper with the story of another man's son, now a member of the Little League. These men were with her all week long, and they knew it. Ellen didn't have any grand ambitions about solving everyone's problems, or keeping them all out of future crime. She didn't give the prisoners any sermons on what they should have done in the past, and said very little of what they must do in the future. She simply tried to help each one to understand himself a little better, to make the best of a bad situation, and to get from one week to the next in one piece.

Ellen is a volunteer *extraordinaire*. I will tell you more about her not only because she is an outstanding person, though quite unknown to the world, but because, through her, I can tell you a few more things you ought to know before you try to enter a prison.

The Qualities of a Volunteer

The story of Ellen answers the two most frequent questions I hear about volunteering in prisons: "How can I help?" and "What talents do I need?"

First of all, there comes a point at which you have to stop

talking about the problems of crime and prisons and prisoners, get off your duff, and go do something about it. That's how you help, and that's what Ellen did. She filled out an application for volunteers at the prison nearest her home. The security staff checked her out to make sure she didn't have a prison record or a relative in the prison, which she didn't. So she was cleared, given identification, and told when she could come. Then she came. No *ifs, ands, buts,* or *maybes.* She came, and she came faithfully.

Secondly, Ellen had the talent most needed in prisons. You have no doubt heard, and will continue to hear, of all the professional skills we need in prisons—professionals like doctors, dentists, lawyers, psychiatrists, teachers, artists, and so on, all people with very specific skills. I, too, have emphasized such needs in the previous chapter. And it is a solemn truth that people with specialized skills are needed in prisons.

Ellen didn't have any of those special skills. How could she? At a young age, she had married a rather sickly fellow who died early in the marriage and left her with nothing but her own resources to raise their child. She survived by working as a clerk for a large insurance company, and now the child was raised and gone. After all those years, Ellen was still a clerk, with limited skills.

But Ellen had a simple, human warmth and caring for other people, and she could make each man feel his own worth. She knew how to reach to the depths of the prisoners as few of the more skilled professionals do. She had a talent as a human being that cannot be learned in school, that cannot be taught or bought, and that is not limited to any profession.

Don't permit any professional or so-called correctional expert to tell you that a specific profession is needed in prisons, to the exclusion of quite ordinary persons. It simply is not true. Most prisoners are people whom nobody cared about from the time they were very small, and plain human kindness and concern are the first of their needs. This concern makes a man survive from one week to the next. There are too many good people like Ellen who feel they would not qualify for prison work because they lack a specific talent, and although this is not true, it may be part of the reason that, in many ways, Ellen is not typical of the average volunteer.

Statistical studies show us that the majority of volunteers come from white, middle-class, relatively secure backgrounds. Most are Protestant by religion and ethic and have a very strong set of religious values. They tend to have an education considerably higher than the national average. And, since they come mostly from businesses and professions, they are also economically comfortable. Contrary to what the man on the street might think, most prison volunteers are not little old ladies (or men) who have nothing else to do but spend their time performing good deeds, like so many Girl Scouts. Most of them are relatively young, the majority are men, and they are busy men with little time to spare. They make the time for these voluntary activities because they are idealistic people who want to help others get some of the same chances in life they have had. They are successful in the world's eyes, and they generally believe that other people can be taught the means to success.[1]

Ellen didn't fit a single aspect of the statistical average, but she was a fine and beautiful person. I wish we had many more like her.

I must point out another difference between Ellen and the average volunteer: she had no problem becoming one. She worked in a minimum-security institution which had an extensive volunteer program already in existence. The personnel were quite accustomed to volunteers, and there was no longer any resistance to them. In fact, their worth was recognized so much that certain members of the staff actively sought more volunteers. It was after a staff member's speech at a church supper that Ellen had volunteered, and the process was pretty simple.

However, one should not expect this to be the case in most prisons. I wish I could say flatly that there are certain kinds of prisons where you are welcome and certain kinds where you aren't. But unfortunately, it isn't that simple. Generally, it is fair to say that you will find a greater degree of acceptance in low- or minimum-security prisons, such as the one Ellen went to, than you will in maximum-security penitentiaries. Still, it isn't all that cut and dried. You will find minimum-security institutions in which you are not permitted, never mind welcomed.

You may even have difficulty determining which institutions are maximum security and which are minimum. Usually, a minimum-security prison is one which houses misdemeanants—people who are serving rather short sentences for relatively minor crimes. But "minimum security" may also refer to a camp that houses people who have nearly finished very long sentences for very serious crimes. The camp may be considered a step in the direction of limited freedom for those who are near release and must become readjusted to normal life; it is almost a half-way house, but not quite.

Maximum-security institutions generally house those inmates convicted of felonies, or serious crimes. Most people in a maximum-security prison are serving fairly long sentences, though some of them may be as short as one or two years. The maximum-security prison is often called a penitentiary or a prison, but it may also be called a correctional institution. A lot of hairsplitting goes on about the differences between these differently labeled places, but in states which call a spade a spade, the state pen is the maxi and the house of correction is the mini.

To confuse matters thoroughly for the uninitiated, there are about eight states which insist on calling all their prisons correctional institutions. I suppose this is very nice in theory, but in practice it means very little except that you can't tell which is maxi and which is mini until you learn a little more about the entire system.

Unhappily, due to the general public attitude toward *all* prisoners, and the usual panic at news of any escape, security mania and the consequent security regulations described in chapter 1 may be just as great in a minimum-security prison as they are in the maximum. Security mania exists in all penal institutions, and the differences between maximum- and minimum-security prisons are merely a matter of degree. But the degree very much influences the welcome volunteers will receive.

The attitude toward volunteers also changes from time to time within any given institution as changes occur in the administration. The warden or superintendent sets the general tone, and the only way to find out what that tone is, and whether you are welcome, is to apply for entrance. In seeking the appropriate avenue of entrance, there are three main kinds of situations you may encounter.

The Avenues of Entrance

The first avenue of entrance is the easiest of all. In some states there is a large and vital volunteer organization that actively seeks volunteers. For instance, the M-2 Program in Washington State, which has now extended to other parts of the West, has been written up in popular magazines like *Reader's Digest*. The state of Minnesota has a headquarters for prison volunteers that you can call to make a date for an interview. In such areas, you may well hear the director of volunteers speak to a church group or a local club. In a few rare instances, if the state is seeking volunteers with specialized skills, you may read an advertisement in a newspaper.

The state of North Carolina has a program through which they try to match volunteers and prisoners of similar interests. After a "getting to know you" period, the volunteer is encouraged to take the prisoner out on a day leave. Within some limits, the two may go off to engage in fishing, baseball, or whatever their hobbies happen to be.

But only a few states are as well organized as these, where they make the entrance easy for you. A few more (for example, Massachusetts and Maryland) are trying to set up similar systems, and may actually have them in full operation by the time this book is printed.

The second main avenue of entrance is via a program within an individual prison. You may find an individual prison with a well-organized volunteer program through which volunteers are actively sought. However, most prisons do not have very well-organized volunteer programs, even though most of them do have activities in which volunteers can participate. You may have read or heard of such a program. However, if it is very casually or poorly organized, the personnel at the prison may not think of it as a "program" at all.

I interviewed an administrator at one of the medium-security federal prisons that I suspected would have a volunteer program. Almost right away he told me they had no program.

"Do you mean to tell me that you don't allow *any* volunteers in an institution this size?" I asked.

"Oh, sure we do," he replied quickly. "Well, we have a Jaycees chapter and AA and people who give courses. And there's a drama group that comes in. You mean that kind of thing?"

Of course, I meant that kind of thing. He had greeted me with the administrator's traditional reserve, since he wasn't quite sure who I was or what I might want to write about "his" prison. But, as he opened up and began to relax, I discovered the prison had over a dozen different kinds of volunteer activities. To be sure, they weren't organized under an umbrella that could be called a "volunteer program," but they were there, and some of them were very good. More important, the activities offered a variety of ways for prisoners to keep in contact with the outside world and for the community to learn about the prison and people in it.

The activities of this prison, which had "no program," included: Jaycees, Alcoholics Anonymous, Gambler's Anonymous, outside drug groups that rapped with the men inside, a drama club, musical bands, visiting sports teams which played against the prisoners' teams, law students who helped with legal advice, university students who gave college-level courses, a few well-educated inmate volunteers who gave courses, discussion groups run by the chaplain, a lecture series, a class in yoga, and outside groups which donated materials for crafts and hobbies. There may have been even more activities, but these came off the top of the administrator's head once he got going. Yet many people in the community didn't know about these activities at all, for they are never advertised. Participation is usually a matter of one volunteer telling a friend or neighbor—strictly word of mouth.

If you have heard of a program, but received the "we don't have a volunteer program" response, it usually means that volunteers are permitted into the prison, but the program is not highly organized. In such cases, I suggest you ask exactly the same question I did. Generally, you will get a similar response because few prisons are willing to admit these days that they don't permit any outsiders. If you get the desired response, stay on the line and try to get the proper and full name of the individual in charge of the volunteer program. In some cases it may be the chaplain; in others, the educational director or the sports director or whoever happens to be available for the job.

If the person in charge of volunteer activities is not immediately available (and no one is on duty twenty-four hours a day), thank the officer to whom you do speak and ask if you may have his name also. Then write it down. The next day or so, when you reach the desired person, tell him that you spoke to Officer Jones on Wednesday and he suggested you call. This immediately indicates not only that this is your second call, but that you seem to know what you are about. It also indicates that, should you fail to get any action on your application, you are keeping a record which someone may have to answer for in the future.

In prisons, record-keeping is a well-respected art which, in spite of my tendencies to the contrary, I have learned can be most useful. Indeed, in many cases, if there is no record, the administrators believe that nothing occurred. So, if you get the runaround, write down the date, to whom you spoke, and what was said. Usually, this will bring results, even though they may not be as quick as you might desire.

Of course, these avenues of entrance may be closed to you if your interest in this field is so new you haven't the foggiest notion of whether or not the prison near you has a program in which you could take part. In this case, you don't yet know anyone who is directly involved, you don't know what the local situation regarding volunteers is, and you don't know quite where to begin. If you are in this position—and many people are—don't call the prison. You are not ready to go there. If your interest is sincere, you can easily take a little time, do a bit of digging, and become minimally informed before you apply for entrance in a volunteer program.

Gathering knowledge about the world of prisons and the whole field of corrections is done the same way, initially, as in any other field, except that accurate information is sometimes a little more difficult to find. Many small libraries didn't stock books on this subject until recently, but most of them are beginning to do so; and in the past many newspapers didn't report on prison conditions unless there was a riot, but this is also changing. Citizen organizations, college students, law schools, the Bar Association, and groups of self-help ex-convicts are all actively engaged in changing the old conditions. A self-help drug group or Alcoholics Anonymous almost always has members who have either visited the prison and know something of the conditions there or members who have been inmates themselves. A really good news reporter is often better than a detective at gathering information. If you know of a local reporter who has been writing about prisons, he or she will be an invaluable source of information.

If you don't even know where the prison is located, the local police, the district attorney's office, or the local judge can tell you. They have all had contacts with the prison, but except for telling you where it is and who the warden is, these people are often poor sources of information. Most policemen and judges, and even some district attorneys, have never set foot inside the prisons to which they send so many offenders.

The appendix of this book contains a list of the major sources of information about volunteer organizations. Check to see whether one of these is near you, or write to them asking for information about local programs. They are glad to disseminate whatever information they have. Also, read at least one or two of the books listed in the appendix. These will give you more detailed knowledge of matters I can only sketch out for you in a work of this kind.

By the time you have read a little, watched the local papers, and listened to others who know something about the corrections system, most likely you will have discovered either an organization or an individual who can introduce you to the prison world or even the prison warden. Clearly the best way to begin your work as a volunteer is with someone who knows the system and the people in it. In this way, you meet the staff not as a stranger who might possibly be suspect until he has proven his worth, but as a friend who will give help and support. You and the staff will feel more comfortable together, and the mutual sense of confidence will create better communication. Without the cooperation of the staff you can do very little, and with it you have a good chance to put your talents to their maximum use in helping prisoners and, eventually, in making the system of justice better for everyone.

Woman's Place

There is, in many institutions, another major obstacle to entry as a volunteer, one that Ellen did not have to worry about. This obstacle is the fact of being a woman. While it may sound strange to the uninitiated and infuriating to those who believe that men and women are equal, the problems encountered by female volunteers are facts to be faced, and they have their roots in a long tradition based on law.

All states require that male and female prisoners be separately maintained, and this requirement makes a good deal of sense. The separation of the sexes started as an eighteenth-century prison reform; prior to that time, men, women, and children were all thrown into prison together. Considering the fact that they not only stole from other prisoners but beat, raped, and sometimes killed one another, the creation of separate facilities for each group was indeed a blessing. The reform prevented male prisoners from taking advantage of women and children. Further, so that male guards could not take unfair advantage of women who were incarcerated, female matrons were assigned to work with female prisoners. Of course, male guards have always been needed for male inmates because of the greater physical strength of men.

At any rate, during the course of the last two hundred years or so, the tradition of separating the sexes became so entrenched that the separation is now considered one of the articles of faith in the field of corrections. At this writing, there is a co-ed prison experiment being conducted at the federal institution in Fort Worth, Texas. But that experiment remains a dream in the fantasy lives of most prisoners across the country, and a foreboding nightmare to most prison administrators. Usually, in male prisons (which are the majority) the nurses in the infirmary, the librarians, cooks, counselors, and teachers all have to be men. And the volunteers must also be male. The converse is true in prisons for women. Even outside the prison, in probation and parole departments, the general rule of thumb is that men work with men, women with women, and the thought of mixing the two is considered utterly scandalous by most correctional personnel.

The overall result of this absolute separation of the sexes has been to double the abnormal aspects of prison life: the confinement and regimentation of a prison being the first abnormal aspect; the absence of the other half of the human race being the second. Relationships with people of the opposite sex, whether they are casual or intimate, whether they are in the home or in business or in our own neighborhoods, are such a normal, ordinary part of life that it seems quite ridiculous to have to mention it. Even voluntary celibates relate to people of the opposite sex on some level. Yet, what has always been, is now, and always will be such a normal part of our existence that we don't even think about it becomes a source of enormous preoccupation inside prisons because of its very absence.

Exclusion of volunteers of the opposite sex prohibits close and meaningful relationships between the sexes. Any frequent contacts foster a suspicion that something more than a platonic friendship may ensue and that that "something" might end in a scandal of sorts. Also, except in the most mature person, separation from the other sex does damage to the self-image and retards inner, personal growth. We must see ourselves reflected in the eyes of both sexes. We need warm, close ties with persons male and female. Finally, separation creates a tremendous temptation to homosexuality. Without making any moral judgment on those who choose homosexuality as a pattern of life, it can be said that such acts are particularly harmful, guilt-ridden, and therefore emotionally damaging to those who are normally heterosexual. In sum, the negative effects of forced separation far outweigh any of the problems which *might* occur as a result of a little judicious mixing of the sexes. Or, at least, so it seems to me.

The problem to consider is not really whether but how to promote that judicious mixture within the confines of a monstrous structure like a prison. A few prisons are experimenting with the novelty of admitting volunteers of the opposite sex, but we can safely estimate that most prisons continue to adhere rather strictly to the old prohibition. Since most prisons are for men, this means primarily a prohibition against women in the field of corrections.

The reason for strict adherence to the old philosophy was very succinctly expressed by one prison guard who had just been informed that women volunteers were to be introduced in his prison. He said, in a low moan, "My God, this is the end." Obviously, he regarded this as something akin to a woman deliberately entering the men's locker room or the cloister of a monastery: deeds that strike terror in the souls of men. It is an invasion of the male sanctuary which provokes the most primitive reactions.

Correctional officials express their thinly disguised terror of women in protective terms. "A woman might be raped or held hostage," but no one can cite an instance of this ever happening. "Well, she might overhear some bad language." Or, "Women are a security problem." I have never understood this last reaction, but I have heard it expressed. Another protest is, "It just isn't right to bring decent women in here," the presumption apparently being that men in prison are too deranged, immoral, or incorrigible to merit the occasional company of a "decent" woman. Lastly, the presence of the fair sex appears to many male prison officials as a distinct pleasure to which convicted offenders, who are being punished, do not have the right.

Because of these attitudes, which sometimes seem burned into the souls of male prison officials, women volunteers should not be surprised to encounter either resistance, hostility, or outright rejection. The woman who is incapable of either overcoming or ignoring these attitudes should work with female offenders until the atmosphere in male institutions becomes more propitious. But in no case should women cease trying to change this situation, simply because there is resistance.

There will always be resistance to change, but quite a number of prison administrators are beginning to see the necessity for it and are quietly beginning to admit volunteers of both sexes. In some areas, the law prohibits administrators from employing women to work with men, and vice versa, but as far as I know, the law usually says nothing about admitting volunteers of both sexes.

However, women remain scarce in most male prisons, and their right to be there at all, whether as staff members or volunteers, is yet to be firmly established. Therefore, wisdom dictates that women who are able to enter male prisons be particularly circumspect in all their words and deeds. Unfair as it may seem, it continues to be a truism in this profession that women must prove their worth while presenting no significant problems or inconvenience to the male majority.

In some places, women are proving their worth and are not a problem, although there are some short-lived discomforts for both sexes. For example, the woman who enters a male preserve must expect to be regarded initially as something of a curiosity. One might just as well send a chimpanzee marching down the hall, so surprised are the men to see the female of our species. They may giggle, or you may feel twenty sets of eyes boring through your back as they stare at the unfamiliar sight. You may also feel swamped with the amount of attention you get, to which you are quite unaccustomed in the normal world. This attention is not due to any special powers or attractions for which you may claim credit, so don't let it go to your head. If at first the inmates trip over themselves to see who can open the door for you, it is only because you are unusual. Once they get used to you, you can open the door for yourself as you always did.

For prisoners, adjustments to female volunteers are similar but more far-reaching. They soon discover that you are talking with them in order to accomplish something specific and not because they look like God's gift to women. They tend to clean up their language, their manners, their bodies, and their clothes more often when women are around. More important, some of the inmates discover that cleaning themselves up is a nice thing to do because it makes them feel better. Some feel like decent men again because a woman accepts them, not as deranged animals, but as human beings who are worthy of her company.

Of course, people who feel good about themselves also tend to behave better. At the prison where I volunteer, some of the very officers who were most apprehensive when women volunteers first arrived on the scene have since told me they see considerably less tension in the prison since women became a regular part of the programs. There is a concomitant decrease in the level of violence among inmates, and the few fistfights that do occur never take place when women are present. The whole tone of the prison is more civilized. Also, the decision to permit women to enter enabled the administration to utilize the abilities of a whole new group and increased the total volunteer power, energy, and talent.

In the volunteer area a pattern can be set which can eventually change the laws that restrict women in prison work and possibly open up careers in an area that has been traditionally restricted to men. If women can function well as counselors, teachers, nurses, doctors, and lawyers, working with both men and women outside prison walls, there is no logical reason why they can't do the same inside; and if they can function on a volunteer basis in prisons, there is no logical reason why some of them cannot do the same work on a paid basis. A few are beginning to do that.

One inmate I know of was almost illiterate, although he never admitted it, and he firmly rejected a counselor's suggestion that he spend his time taking a course in basic adult education. The very next day he reversed his decision when he discovered that a rather attractive woman tutored the men individually in reading. The reasons for this reversal were written all over his face, though, of course, he staunchly insisted that he had seen the light and was really going to improve himself this time around.

Now one can look back and say, "Who cares *why* he took the course." Six months later his reading ability had improved by three grade levels, and he had completed the first book he had ever read in his life. There were other firsts for him: he got the first sustained attention he had ever received, experienced his first sense of accomplishment; and had the first inkling that what he was, what he did, and what he became really did matter to someone. Does it matter, really, that the someone was a woman to whom he was attracted?

I once discussed the presence of female volunteers with a group of inmates after they had become accustomed to it. "You have women participating in all the same activities as male volunteers, except sports. You're used to them now and you can see that they're not doing anything very different from the men. So, really, what difference does it make whether or not they are here?"

"Yeah. Well. When you put it that way, I dunno what to say. But I'll tell ya. I'd rather have you sittin' there than your husband any day!" A pause for thought. "One thing is—a lotta guys don't participate in nothin'. They don't improve themselves. Don't want to. I seen some of them come into a group jus' to see the women. Then after a while they start to get involved in the group." That's the difference it makes.

At a time when many correctional administrators are beginning to wake up to the value of having female volunteers in prisons, many of the women who are qualified to play a useful role are rejecting volunteer work of any kind. They reject it on the theory that volunteer work is a male-chauvinist method of keeping women off the job market. They also feel that if an administrator seriously believes a job is worth doing, he ought to be willing to pay for it. Further, they say that if women simply stopped volunteering the millions of hours of work they presently give to society, organizations would have to find the money to pay them for their services.

There is both truth and fallacy in these statements. Women have been grossly used as a source of cheap labor, and they have worked for no pay in jobs that ought to be paying jobs. But I believe many volunteer tasks would not be performed by paid personnel if we all refused to do volunteer work. The jobs would simply not be done at all, and many needed services would be nonexistent.

In prisons, 95 percent or more of the budget is spent on security and maintenance. In many places it is 100 percent. And in most instances, administrators must do battle regularly with the legislature in order to get the money they have. Legal aid, counseling, education, libraries, and athletic facilities, the services that prisoners need most, either receive short shrift or are nonexistent. Even without such services, the average yearly cost to the taxpayer for keeping a person in prison ranges from $6,000 to $12,000, depending on whether the inmate has a family on welfare.

Anyone who believes that taxpayers will tolerate increased costs for prison services is a dreamer. And anyone who believes that administrators will reallocate available funds from security to services hasn't learned much about prisons or what society expects of them. So long as we continue to have prisons, our money will be spent on security and maintenance.

Therefore, so long as we have our fortresses, we will need volunteers—men *and* women—who can bring a little human caring and hope to those inside the walls. In the last analysis, it matters little whether volunteers are men or women, but it is better to have both. It doesn't matter whether they are housewives who have a morning to spare when the children are in school or executives who can give only two hours a month, whether they are bright young college kids trying to comprehend the meaning of crime and tragedy or old folks who can give the wisdom of age and experience. It's important only that volunteers come not for the money, but for joining human beings together.

Suiting Your Needs

Ellen was also fortunate because the prison in which she volunteered had a variety of programs and a person with almost any kind or level of talent could find a place in one of them. Most prisons don't offer such a variety, and you may need to find out not only what programs are available, but whether you can or want to participate in them.

For example, one institution may be attempting to launch an education program in which volunteer teachers are needed. If you are a teacher, you will be welcome. However, if you teach regularly during the day, you may not want to do the same kind of work in your free time. Don't let anyone push you into a slot that you don't like.

I know of a man who volunteered in the same Fellowship program that Ellen was in. He was a well-trained, educated librarian, and this was known to the administration. Thus, when there was a temporary shortage of volunteers for the prison library, he was approached to help fill the gap. He flatly refused because he felt he needed a change of pace from his ordinary work. His wishes were respected, the issue was dropped, and he remained in Fellowship, which is where he wanted to be.

The administration was wise not to press this man; an unhappy volunteer is a volunteer who will soon disappear. And volunteers have every right to perform a service they enjoy, not simply one to which they are driven by pangs of guilt. Some administrators will attempt to direct you into work they happen to need done at the moment, whether or not it is what you want to do. For this reason, it is wise to assess yourself and your needs in advance, and be fairly definite if there is anything specific you do or do not wish to join in.

Of course, for some people, work is not a task to be finished with. For a happy few, their work and their happiness are the same thing, and they never seem to tire of using their special talents. These are the people whose work is literally an expression of themselves. If you are one of these fortunate persons, all you have to do is find out whether your talent can be used in the prison.

I can think of only a few hobbies—such as gun collecting, or anything else connected with the martial arts—that are forbidden in a prison. Most arts and professions are not forbidden, but their usefulness is sometimes questioned simply because they are unfamiliar to prison administrators. For example, officials might be puzzled about how an architect would apply his talent in a prison, or what a circus performer would teach. If you have a talent, profession, or hobby that is not generally used in prisons, it may take a bit of courage on your part to put it to work. You may even have to start an entire program of your own. Starting a program from scratch requires specific talents, which not everyone has, but it can be done.

Starting Your Own Program

Martha and Elliot Rothman, two architects from Boston, told me they worried needlessly for several months about whether their professional services would be rejected or ridiculed if they offered them at the county prison. They had long been concerned about prison conditions and felt that they could help at least in changing the grim atmosphere, even if they could not change all the other evils of prison. So they did something that most people would not do.

They decided to stop worrying about anticipated reactions and finally just called the sheriff to tell him they would like an opportunity to see whether it was possible to apply their professional expertise to improve the prison. To their surprise, they received an invitation to look the place over and make suggestions.

During the course of the next two years, they wrought more changes in one prison than any other two people I have ever heard about. Not only did they radically change the appearance of the prison, but, more important, they contributed in large measure to a change in the spirit of the place.

The work to be done in the prison was extensive and potentially very expensive, even though the Rothmans were donating their time, and the budget was so small it could barely be seen with a magnifying glass. However, these problems were surmounted. The Rothmans canvassed the inmate population for men who would like to work with architects, conducted a small class in drafting and design, and provided professional supervision and guidance while the inmates themselves developed plans for physical changes in the prison. Inmate labor executed the plans and the only money required from the budget was for two-by-fours, plasterboard, and paint. There were many advantages to this program, in addition to the physical alterations that created a more humane atmosphere with little money.

First, there was the potential for changing the inmates' and volunteers' attitudes and behavior. The Rothmans represented a level of professional society, of competence and social conscience, that few of the inmates had ever encountered. In turn, as volunteers they had a new opportunity to understand the offenders' society. The Rothmans involved other professionals and student architects in the program, and the inmates engendered enthusiasm among their fellow prisoners. The program gave the inmates a chance to affect the appearance of their environment and involved them to a greater extent in influencing management decisions. It opened and exercised the imagination of the men and gave them a level of responsibility most had never had before.

Inmate-staff relationships were also affected—in two ways. The process of planning new facilities fostered understanding and cooperation as the inmates held necessary meetings with supervisory personnel. The staff began to see that inmates could handle responsibility and could be given the opportunity to make many decisions without ill effects on the security or order of the prison.

The program also gave the inmates involved the joy of seeing a job well done, and it opened career opportunities for several men. Two gifted members of the group, both of whom had no career plans when they entered prison, are now working for an architectural firm and studying to become architects themselves. Another is in drafting; several others are in construction. One may have a career in art, and another is painting houses. So far, none has returned to prison.

In two years, many works were accomplished. A shop for manufacturing brooms was turned into four bright, cheerful classrooms now in use daily. A large, open, unused area was turned into eight small offices for private counseling, testing programs, and legal counseling. The large, dreary recreation room was partitioned into four areas—two for TV watchers, two for activities such as chess, cards, checkers, puzzles, and other games —and one section now contains a submarine-sandwich shop

owned and operated by the inmates. Next to the recreation
room, a storeroom and office were turned into a very pleasant library.

Almost every corner of the prison was repainted in loud,
vibrant colors. The visiting room, instead of institutional green,
is now bright yellow, punctuated by colorful posters. The
infirmary was rearranged and reequipped by the staff and
painted by inmates to make a more healthful atmosphere. The
former "auditorium," which was used only for religious services,
and little used for that, was turned into a gym, which is probably
the most frequented place in the prison. The cell blocks are now
a series of contrasting colors seen in one glance. Colors inside
each cell are determined by the man who occupies it; some are
bright, some dark, and others have murals of considerable beauty
or humor on the walls. If a new inmate does not like the taste of
the former occupant, he may repaint, but he must do all the
work himself. In any case, the decisions about his living space
are his own. The inmates, architects, and the prison won a cita-
tion from *Progressive Architecture* for their design of the dining
room—one out of only eighteen awards granted to major architectural projects across the nation. So popular and productive
has the program been, that the Rothmans finally obtained a
grant that pays one-half the salary of a full-time art and architecture teacher. The Rothmans pay the other half.

It must be agreed that what Martha and Elliot Rothman accomplished was singular and dramatic, viewed from any angle.
And while I don't think that everyone can or should run out and
do just what they did, I think it is useful to look at their accomplishments and witness what can occur when imagination and
determination are applied.

They are very modest when questioned about their work,
and will tell you that the inmates really did the design and construction work, while they offered guidance and direction; they
will say that the program's success was possible because of a
cooperative administration. What they won't tell you is that
none of the changes would have occurred at all if they hadn't
been able to apply great creative talent and imagination to a
minuscule budget. The Rothmans won't remind you that archi-

tects are accustomed to working with wealthy clients or that the services they rendered without pay were worth many thousands of dollars, quite beyond my calculating abilities. They won't tell you that one of their most gifted inmate-students was also an escape artist who almost wrecked the architectural program or mention how much time they spend keeping in touch with their ex-students, placing them in jobs, or helping them enroll in school for further education.

Nor will the Rothmans dwell on the problems they had to surmount. In addition to lack of money, they had to deal with a staff that for quite some time regarded their projects as crazy, who thought their program was "coddling" prisoners, and who presented continuing objections based on security considerations. The Rothmans' patience, diplomacy, and willingness to work around security problems finally won out, so they are now well accepted by the staff. Furthermore, most staff members now point with pride to the difference between theirs and other prisons.

The Rothmans are exceptional people, there is no doubt. And, as they are the first to point out, they are part of an exceptional team effort which combines volunteers, inmates, staff, and administration. The volunteer program in this prison is built on a philosophy and directed toward specific goals, but remains open about how those goals are to be achieved. It is one that accepts new ideas and proposals with a "let's give it a try" attitude. Through either staff, volunteer, or inmate initiative, or a combination of all three, the institution encompasses every one of the models mentioned in the previous chapter, plus other more experimental programs not mentioned at all and some that are still in the planning stages.

I regret to say that the prison in which the Rothmans worked is not typical. Many institutions are strict lockups, punitive institutions in which any talk of "corrections" or "rehabilitation" is nothing more than a sick joke. Some prisons wouldn't meet the most basic standards of sanitation, never mind having programs to help the minds and spirits of prisoners.[2]

You may well find a prison which has either no volunteer programs at all or one which has one or two programs, such as an

AA, into which you do not fit. If you encounter this situation, you have two choices as a volunteer. First, you can volunteer in another area of social need. Second, you can try to do something about the situation by launching a volunteer program in the prison.

I would not fault anyone who chose the first path, because the second one is obviously difficult and certainly is not practical for most of us. But just in case you are one of those with boundless courage and would like to start a volunteer program, let us review a few factors you should keep in mind. You should know exactly what you want to do in the program, how to do it, and whether you have the resources to carry it out. You must know your own business (for example, the Rothmans knew architecture and how to teach it) and how your area of interest can satisfy the needs of the prison and the people in it—both inmates and staff. You should have a specific proposal to present to the administration and set clear lines of responsibility in carrying it out. It is helpful to have either some prison experience or a very clear perception of how prisons function and to know the rules within which you must work. Finally, you need the cooperation of the chief administrator of the prison.

Knowing what kind of program you want to start isn't a problem, since it is a rare person who would be foolish enough to start a program in something he knew little or nothing about. For example, I can't imagine the Rothmans trying to start a recreation program. However, I can easily imagine people going wrong on knowing whether their program will meet the needs of those inside the prison, because people tend to think that what they consider important is important to everyone. For example, it would be foolish to try to start a course in architecture in an institution that does not provide basic educational courses in reading and math. It would be silly to try to start a bridge club in a prison where poker is the popular game or to bring a Handel and Haydn concert to a place where everyone is listening only to rock and roll. There isn't much sense in pushing for a library if the number-one priority on the warden's and the prisoners' list is a sports program. Critical needs must be known and satisfied before one can worry about variety; if basic needs go unmet, variety is a luxury.

I'll use the Rothmans again to illustrate how you can plan and propose your program to prison officials. They began their work with the very specific proposal of creating needed classrooms out of the old broom shop. They detailed the materials they needed, the personnel required, and the amount of money it would cost. They also offered good suggestions for overcoming the major problem of funds. They set lines of responsibility about who would do which tasks. Finally, the project had a clear beginning, middle, and end, and there were no *maybes* or pie in the sky. Administrators know that projects that generate hopes in a prison and then fall apart, are simply harbingers of trouble. Therefore, they want reasonable assurance of successful completion before they approve a plan at all.

Absolutely essential in starting any program is knowing how prison rules work—a fact that is poorly understood by many people. It is positively necessary that you be able to work within the rules of the institution and accept the limitations they may place on your project. It takes a certain resignation to put up with restrictive rules and regulations, but if you don't have that quality, you can forget about being the originator of a program.

There was a story in a library journal of three young librarians who were instrumental in assisting the warden of the Allegheny County Jail in Pittsburgh in developing a library. The warden had initiated the project himself, and had already made a library area out of what was formerly a series of eight cells, but he needed professionals to organize a collection.

The three librarians did a very commendable job under difficult circumstances. They were faced with a number of restrictions that are not the least bit unusual in jails and prisons, but would be nightmarish to most librarians. First, the borrowers could not have direct access to the library, but had to choose from a typewritten list of books: no browsing. Also, there could be no paperbacks in the collection. It was to be strictly recreational reading, so there could be no basic educational materials such as textbooks. There were to be no books of a sexually inflammatory nature and none glorifying crime, restrictions that eliminated most popular books, depending on one's interpretation of what is sexually inflammatory and what glorifies crime. In any case, the prisoners were not getting much voice in what they wanted, and good librarians know it's a bad library that doesn't give its customers pretty much what *they* want.[3]

The professionals in this case complied with all the warden's requirements, which was wise. Many volunteers would have started a short-lived but fierce battle over such restrictions, and they would have made a serious tactical error. It is an error frequently made by people who do not understand how prisons function.

You should get into your head the fact that prisoners get pretty much what the administration will allow, unless there's a court order to the contrary. They don't get what the administration doesn't want; it's as simple as that. This principle applies to the "enlightened" prisons of the federal system as well as the little jail run by a sheriff from the back woods.[4]

It is difficult for people outside to comprehend fully the power of prison administrators. But when dealing with prisons, it is something you had better comprehend. If you don't, and if you violate the rules, you will find yourself barred from further entrance, and then all your plans for helping prisoners amount to nothing. I don't suggest that you forsake your ideals about certain rights prisoners should have (such as freedom to read what they want), but I do suggest that you do not display your most intense feelings at first.

I suppose there are many diplomatic ways to handle objections to your ideals, depending on your imagination and skill. I enjoy the memory of one such situation in which I was helping to launch a prison library. There is no rule that says you have to act as I did, but the example can be helpful.

The officer in direct charge of our operation had all kinds of worries about what would be permitted on the library shelves. Since we had several inmates interested in art, I brought in an art history book I had used as a textbook in college—a very acceptable book in the art world to which I could conceive no objection. But the officer felt differently. He said, "Do you realize there are some nudes in that?" and flipped the book open to several different pages that, sure enough, had nude or nearly nude figures by famous artists such as Botticelli, Picasso, and Michelangelo. Though the officer acknowledged that they were classic and beautiful, he did not think it was good for the inmates. And the inmates had never before been able to get anything that he did not think was good for them. He considered this book sexually inflammatory, so he promptly confiscated it.

I acquiesced in the situation partly because I was shocked and couldn't believe what was happening, and partly because I could see no alternative except quitting the program, which I was too stubborn to do. After six months of discussion, I finally convinced the officer that the art history book was perfectly acceptable reading for anyone, including prison inmates. I have to admit that I nagged him a little, since I pursued the question every time I saw him, but I always stopped short of being thrown out of the program. I don't think he was ever really convinced of the rightness of my position, but he did get tired of talking about the matter.

Michelangelo finally won out, but he might have been permanently ostracized from the library (and me with him) if I had forced the issue at my first meeting with the officer. And if his actions strike you as being oppressive or strange or funny, don't laugh too soon. Incidents of this kind are everyday affairs in prisons, and you are sure to come across a few of them if you work in a prison.

Other kinds of restrictions may be placed on you, depending on what sort of program you plan to develop, and there is not much you can do about them except to go along with them or find adequate solutions. Though it may seem discouraging at first, nothing beats the feeling of joy you have when a problem is finally solved. The fewer problems you cause, the more successful your program will be, and everyone from the newest prisoner to the oldest warden will benefit in the long run.

To launch any program successfully, you must be able to convince the chief administrator of the prison that your program is a good idea, since prisons function on very authoritarian lines of responsibility. The top man sets the tone of the entire institution, and your success or failure in reaching him is a good indicator of the success or failure of your program.

The top officials are known by a variety of titles, but most often they are called superintendents or directors. In old-fashioned prisons, they may still be called wardens. And, in county institutions, the man you need to reach is often the sheriff. Whatever name the official totes, he's not a man to ignore if you are starting a program and aiming for success.

If he seeks your aid, as in the case of the young librarians I mentioned, you don't have a problem. But if you are the initiator of a new program, you may have to convince him of the efficacy of your ideas. And to sell your ideas to the warden you must be perceptive enough to figure out an approach that will be effective with him. I can offer you only a few clues: the rest is up to you.

Your ability to sell the idea depends on the kind of institution the warden wants. Once you discover what kind of prison he wants, no matter what your personal philosophy or reasons for starting the program, you have to concentrate on what he wants and what his attitudes are. Otherwise, you are finished before you start. There are several attitudes you may find in top officials, and for each one there is a corresponding selling pitch.

One type of warden, who is very common, is the one who simply wants to run a peaceful, quiet, efficient institution in which nobody gives anyone else any trouble. In fact, many wardens consider themselves successful if they never have any riots or trouble. The good prisoner, to them, is a quiet one, regardless of his crime, length of sentence, or whether he will live a decent, successful life when he gets out of prison. He is good if he doesn't cause headaches. This attitude is based on the fact that the warden usually never hears from the public or the legislature or anyone else except when there is trouble in the prison. He may never get any compliments for those inmates he has managed to help, but he will get a lot of complaints and may lose his job if there are too many disturbances in his prison.

If you suspect this is the warden's attitude, the basic selling point you must make is that the program you wish to start is going to contribute to a greater degree of peace within the prison. Prisons, by their very nature, will never be very peaceful places. Whenever you put a large number of reasonably healthy, physically and mentally active people in one place—people who don't want to be there in the first place—and give them little to do but sit in their cells and dream of ways of causing trouble, the chances are very good that you will have a lot of trouble. A sports facility, recreational program, or library can help young prisoners work off the physical energy they build up or give them the intellectual stimulation they need. This is not "coddling" prisoners, but it is a way of preventing madness and violence. It makes the institution safer for the prisoners who must live there and for the staff who work there—a good selling point with a warden who wants peace and quiet.

Another problem that many wardens worry about is the morale of their staff—more than the morale of their inmates. Since prisons are rather depressing places in which to work, and since the work is difficult at best, maintaining staff morale is always a problem. Whether or not it is fair, the fact is that the public image of prison personnel is absolutely abominable. Many volunteers think only of what they can do for the inmates, and some go overboard in their contempt for the guards. This attitude leaves the guards in a very unrewarding position, and when they feel it, morale goes down. When staff morale is very low, the prison is headed for troubles, and every good warden knows this.

If you think staff morale is one of the warden's concerns— and the chances are good that it is—you have another selling point. Every employee likes to work in a place that he can feel some pride in; it's good for his morale. A good workman in a shoe factory likes to feel that his company makes shoes of the highest quality, since it makes him feel like a better workman. Prison personnel like to feel that their prison is, if not the best in the country or state, at least one of the best-run places. If you can show the warden that the program you have in mind is going to boost morale in the whole institution, he is likely to view your effort favorably.

A third possible selling point for your program is its effect on the image of the warden himself. Some wardens don't care about what the public thinks of them. Some may even gruffly state that they know they are doing a good job, and they don't care what anyone thinks of them personally. But don't believe it —at least, in nine cases out of ten, don't believe it. Everyone likes to be well thought of, and any person who can run a peaceful institution that also has good programs is well thought of. If you can get this truth across to a reluctant warden, you have removed your most serious obstacle. If you cannot remove this obstacle, you might as well not try to proceed.

But, being somewhat of an optimist, I'm hoping you have either the good sense and courage to face these obstacles in selling your program or the good fortune to be able to avoid them. I mention them not to discourage you, but to prepare you for what you might not have expected.

The obstacles encountered in entering a prison or getting a program started are only the beginning; the greater challenge of working directly with inmates and staff lies ahead. No one really knows how to solve all the problems that bring men and women to prison, and no one knows quite how to change a criminal pattern. The unknown is always a little scary, but it is also exciting and challenging. However, you may want to meditate in advance on whether you can handle the relationships we are now going to examine.

The *Wall Street Journal* carried a lead article one day concerning the rights prisoners were seeking through court action. With considerable interest, I read the description of typical cases before the courts until before my wondering eyes appeared the summary of one very curious case.

A group of prisoners had started a new religion and were complaining to the court about the lack of religious freedom in the prison. Their organization was called the Church of the New Song, and among the materials necessary to conduct its liturgy were steak and wine. Some inmate-ministers said they required not just any old wine, but Harvey's Bristol Cream. The complainants demanded not only that their numerous ministers each be paid $16,000 per year as chaplains, but that the prison administration cease restraining their sizable following from participation in the prescribed liturgy.

It has been said that nothing can surpass the piety of the wretched. What decent human being, do you suppose, can bear to witness the anguish these men suffered in the name of heaven? Unhappily for those tortured souls, the prison administration was able to bear the sight without too much distress; it seems the warden did not look kindly on "high" churches.

The ingenious prisoner who founded the nation's newest cult was no doubt a man of humor and a high degree of manipulative skill. He was a con man and knew that there's a sucker born every minute.

4

FOR BLEEDING HEARTS

The irony in this story is that there are many people who will view the case with sufficient seriousness to align themselves with one of the two extreme attitudes which tend to surface in any discussion of crime and criminals. At one extreme is the attitude that there is only one cause of crime: downright evil. What we really need is tougher laws and police, more prisons and more capital punishment. There's one sure way to lower the crime rate: shoot 'em. At the other end of the spectrum is the attitude that all prisoners are political prisoners who are incarcerated because we have a very sick society. All police are pigs, and guards are sadists who enjoy torturing prisoners. Because prisons don't do much good, we don't need them at all.

The problem with both of these attitudes is that they are overly simplistic and ignore reality. The first ignores the reality that violence begets nothing but more violence and terror. It fails to recognize that many people would not be in prison except for the fact that they are poor. Those who espouse this view would probably be the first to want the "law of elimination" tempered if one of their relatives were about to be shot. The second attitude forgets that, to some extent, society has always been sick and probably always will be, but this attitude is poor justification for committing serious crimes. This view does not recognize that there is something within the individual as well as in the society which causes him to violate laws the majority can abide by. This group also fails to recognize that, while the majority of prisoners need not be incarcerated for the sake of our safety, we do need protection from some prisoners.

Because these extremes of opinion don't examine the very complicated realities, they hurt us all in several ways. First, they cut off the communication, the dialogue, between people, without which there is little progress. One side alienates prisoners by condemning them all and denying them any hope; the other alienates staff, who rightly resent doing a hard job and receiving nothing but abuse. Secondly, these attitudes prevent us from dealing with real problems, because we cannot deal with problems unless we can first state them with some objectivity. Neither threatening the prison staff nor seeing no wrong in their treatment of prisoners encourages them to acknowledge and correct what is wrong or to weed out those guards who are sadistic. Similarly, by threatening or overexcusing prisoners, we do not help them try to change what is wrong in their attitudes or behavior. Finally, by failing in objectivity, either extreme leaves us open to failure, hurt, and disillusionment.

Obviously, within the prison, there is little need to worry about the extremist who hates prisoners. He simply does not come near the place because he has no feelings of sympathy which would draw him there. However, since an interest in prisons is very fashionable today, the prison does become a mecca to those who can see in it only a group of fine lads who have, perhaps, sowed their wild oats too publicly. These are the bleeding hearts who will believe in the sincerity of that new religion or, indeed, accept anything a prisoner tells them as gospel.

I worry about the bleeding hearts because they tend to be innocent, naïve, decent people who would never consciously deceive another person. They are basically warmhearted, kind, good people. They are often gentle people for whom we should sincerely thank God because they can love the unlovable, have compassion for the wayward spirit, give hope to the hopeless. They are the friends of the downtrodden, champions of the defeated, finders of the lost. They are also perfect victims for the con artist.

Any volunteer who is bent on working in a prison ought to take a good look in the mirror and acknowledge right away that he fits at least part of the description above, because if you didn't fit at least part of that description, you probably would not consider volunteering in a prison. Once you can be honest enough with yourself to admit that you have a bleeding heart, you have already reached for the tourniquet which will prevent you from being seriously hurt.

There isn't any need to try to change your feelings of sympathy or human pity because without these feelings you would accomplish little good. But perhaps you could try to leave outside the prison gate any slobbering sentimentality about good guys and bad guys and all the popular clichés. The best protection you can provide for yourself, and probably the only protection you will need, is an open mind and open eyes so that you perceive what is really there.

A good coat of protection demands that you see both prisoners and staff as they really are, rather than as you want to dream they are, with some good and some bad in each camp. You will find love and hate, laughter and tragedy. There will be events that will pull at your heartstrings, frustrations that will try your patience, regulations that you want to ignore. A few people will offer you the best that is in them, and some will manipulate your sympathies for very selfish purposes. Some will use you, which is not entirely bad if you are a willing instrument and if you are being used in a way which helps someone and hurts no one.

You will never be quite sure about whether you are really useful and really doing some good unless you perceive when someone is doing a con job on you. I do not suggest that this is an easy thing to know. I've been fooled before, and I'm sure I will be fooled again. Wiser heads than mine have been turned because they were dealing with people who are experts in the game of deception.

What you can do is at least be aware of various levels of deception you are certain to encounter if you spend any length of time as a prison volunteer. Sometimes people will deceive you, and oftentimes you may deceive yourself. Some levels of deception are really quite harmless; others are not so harmless at all.

One of the theological mysteries that always intrigues me is how, in the end, God will manage to dispense perfect justice and mercy and still give us all our comeuppance. Every human controversy seems to end with one disputant feeling he got a bad deal.

A little boy who gives his brother a punch in the eye is sure to feel that punishment for the punch would be unjust because of the circumstances: his brother provoked him and deserved what he got for being a pest. The provoker, naturally, believes that his pestering in no way warranted such measures; he wants straight retributive justice and no mercy. In any case, no matter what the judge decides, it is unlikely that he will please both parties because no judge has yet discovered God's knack.

Prisoners are not unlike the two boys—and the rest of us—in that they tend to feel very often that they got the short end of justice. I've never yet met a prisoner who was willing to say that his punishment was exactly what he deserved; as a volunteer, you are sure to hear many a tale about the miscarriage of justice. My own feeling about these stories is that most of them lie in the gray area which is neither truth nor falsehood.

A few claims of innocence are genuine, and one should keep in mind the fact that our system of justice is administered by fallible human beings who do sometimes accuse and convict the wrong person. All our constitutional safeguards and limits on the powers of the police and the courts exist precisely because we are so prone to error.

However, in most instances, there are multiple meanings behind a prisoner's cry at the lack of justice. He may mean that the circumstances under which he acted have not been given sufficient consideration. For example, "So, I hit him. So what? He called my wife a whore." Like the boy, this prisoner feels he did not deserve punishment for responding to such provocation unless the other man received equal punishment for slander. He has a point. Or an inmate might think the effects of incarceration are so serious that they far outweigh the seriousness of his crime. Depending on the nature of his crime, he may well have a point there also.

A prisoner may feel he is no worse a man and no more dangerous than ten other people who committed the same crime, but did not get caught. The system is unfairly making an example of him in order to deter others who might commit a similar crime—another valid point, which criminologists and philosophers frequently debate.

Finally, he might believe he would have received a lesser punishment if he had been able to afford a good lawyer who could have poked holes in the evidence or found a technical violation in the legal procedure. This is quite likely to be true.

None of these explanations mean that the prisoner did not

commit a crime or that he is innocent as a wet newborn, but they mean that what might seem on the surface of things to be a blatant lie (his avowed innocence), may not be a lie when viewed from the prisoner's position. Decrying justice is simply a prisoner's way of exonerating himself from total responsibility for the unhappy condition he is in.

There are some among the righteous who will disagree with me, but I find little harm in accepting these claims of relative innocence unless they are clearly so far removed from truth that they become lame excuses for a pattern of behavior which is consistently harmful to other people. In many cases, you will never be quite sure of the whole truth, and I think decency dictates that you refrain from recrimination. The past is not past for a person in prison, for the iron bars remind him of it with painful regularity. If a volunteer is to be of much use to the offender, he must concentrate on the future rather than the past. To be of any use to the rest of society, the volunteer should also be aware that past behavior can be prologue to the future, and a failure to recognize the possibility of future crimes is foolhardy.

In addition to the con job a prisoner may try to do on the outsider, he often does an excellent job of deceiving himself.

We all deceive ourselves to some extent so that we do not have to examine or acknowledge responsibility for unpleasant aspects of ourselves. It is simply too destructive for the ego to look in a mirror and say, "What an ugly face." It's much easier to say, "Well, I have the advantage of a very strong chin." We need to support images of ourselves as people who are attractive, interesting, or appealing to others, and our little deceptions give us the self-confidence we need to achieve success, to function well in life.

We often have the arrogance to demand that people in prison examine their inner selves, their attitudes, with far more honesty than we would be able to muster. Facing the real self is always a difficult task, and is especially difficult for the person in prison because he has been publicly labeled, stamped, and processed as a criminal—a human of sorts, but one unfit for anything but a barred cell, a person unworthy of human society. To prevent himself from succumbing to total despair and the destruction of his ego, it may well be necessary for the inmate to scream out, "I'm not bad. I'm not any worse than you." And in order to do this, he may in many ways have to deny, if not his acts, at least responsibility for them; it may be the only way for him to live with himself. The everlasting problem for the volunteer and all correctional personnel is: how do you deter a person from future crime by insisting that he accept responsibility for his acts without asking him to destroy the inner self he now has?

Some people, using criticism and exposure, want to destroy the old self of the prisoner so they can build a new one. But we have no way of knowing whether a new, healthy spirit can be built. Before we open our mouths with criticism, we should remember that the inmate is a human being who may face destruction or salvation depending partly on how he is treated. It may be enough if he considers the notion of responsibility at all, without our asking him to apply it to his own acts. He may be trying to build a self-image strong enough to face the world again or confidence so he can do something right in the future. The prisoner may be in a state of delicate balance, trying to decide his responsibility to others and others' to him. So long as he is not living in a complete dream world, I have grave doubts that anyone should attempt to destroy this delicate balance by robbing the prisoner of all self-deception. It may help him in the long run.

I've often thought the following letter, written by a prisoner to a confused volunteer, explained rather well the problem of self-image and its relationship to the volunteer:

"I find it verry hard to express myself on such an involved subject, but here gos anyway.

"The man I was describing last night was myself and to say the least I don't know verry much about me. These things I can tell you. I was never verry importent in my early life and becouse of this I still find it verry hard to put much faith and trust in myself even today. I fermly belive that one of the most importent things you can do is to make this person feel importent. You will find this a most difficult job because he will trust no one, he will tax youre patients to the upmost limet and then expect even more because, if you are realy his friend you will pull out all the stops just for him. This is what friends are for, to wieght on him hand and foot like servent slaves. He has no idia what so ever what responsabillity is or what it shood be used for yet you will find him, time after time, grasping for and misusing responsabill-ity and athority.

"His word given in solm oth means nothing, yet youer word is allways youre sacred word of oth and there is no posible reson that you should not fite raging hell fire just to prove to him that you are his friend. You are so unimportant that he can see no reason why you would not get up in the middle of the night and walk 10 miles bair foot through a blizzard to give him a sigerette and if you forgot the matches you are in a world of troble. He will expect that you are his friend that you will defend him agenst the world and belive me, the world was created for the sole perpuse of persecuting him——if you don't belive me just ask him.

"One of the most importent things to remember, I think, is that even if he wants verry much to he can not put his trust in you or anyone else for that matter and that includs himself. He will create bad situation after bad situation for himself and not be able to see where he is in any to blame for his delema. He will want to know "why me, how come a millon people do it that way and get away with it and I have get caut, why is it always me.

"He will strik blindly at unjust acts because these unjust acts are agenst him personaly. He will frequently use the high ab-strastions they, everybody and nobody, in which he is also in-cluded. The truble is that he cares verry much, that he belives verry deeply. The truble comes when he can not see where he dose all the bad things to other people that "thay" are not 'spose to do to him.

"The only advice I can give you is to allways be there when he needs a friend (and that is always). If you can show him that the whole world can not be wrong all at once and that his own inability to act in a constructive way insted of blowing up in a pressing situatin, then you can probly convince him to go to a syco-anallist and find out why he has so much truble geting along with people and why he is so unreasonable in his demands on people."

The kinds of conning just described are pretty harmless. Some of this may aid in mending a damaged self-image and be unconsciously designed to make you think well of the prisoner, to make you accept him. This kind of conning may be good if it leads to the development of a person who can accept some responsibility for his future acts, but very often it doesn't.

Unless the prisoner is using conning in a positive way, you would be wise to believe what the prisoner said in his letter: "You are so unimportent" that he will use you as a tool to get what he wants. If you are his friend, you will defend him, forget the rest of the world for him, and do just exactly what he wants. You, somehow, owe it to him; it is your responsibility to "wieght on him hand and foot like servent slaves."

The above is a level of conning that feeds on your sympathy as a bleeding heart and on your guilt, since you are supposed to feel guilty as part of the society which put him in prison. This conning, too, can be harmless enough if you recognize it for what it is and if you don't let it get out of control. It is difficult to draw the controlling line, but you can be certain you have gone beyond it if you begin to receive subtle signals from your friend that he thinks he is the most important person, or the only person, in your life, or that he believes your life should revolve around him. If you are not honest enough to level with him at the first signal you get, one of you is heading for emotional distress and hurt. Some people refuse to receive the signals, not because they are softhearted, but because they are on their own ego trip and enjoy having others dependent on them.

An example of such an ego trip involved Mary and Jim, a young couple who befriended David while he was in prison. David came from a background that would fit any psychologist's description of emotional deprivation, and Mary and Jim were the first people he had ever known who really cared about him, loved him in their own way, responded to him, helped him, and were determined that they would launch him on a new path.

David liked the idea of somebody else launching him, and he grew in confidence partly because he found his first love: Mary. He firmly believed she was in love with him and would later divorce her husband for his sake. Indeed, not having had any real love in his life, he couldn't comprehend any other motive powerful enough to account for her kindness.

Mary and Jim were advised of the gossip circulating about the idea of their divorce, but they did not do enough to convince David his dreams had no basis in reality. They did not really level with him. And in spite of their knowledge of David's intentions, they permitted him to live with them after his release. Six weeks later, David quit his job and disappeared with a large amount of their savings.

The financial loss Mary and Jim suffered was small compared to the disillusionment and despair they felt. David was hurt, too, when he finally accepted the fact that there was to be no divorce and no happily-ever-after marriage to Mary. All this suffering, or at least much of it, could have been avoided if Mary had not been on an ego trip. She couldn't convince David that she wasn't in love with him, because she enjoyed his adoration. Finding that she was attractive to David was actually a support for her ego, which had flagged a little because of a dull life and a rather uninspiring husband. In the end, she felt that she had been used by David, but it seems quite an open question as to who was using whom. Both of them confused love with dependence and both had been building their egos at the expense of the other.

Overdependence is never a good idea because it does not help the prisoner stand on his own feet later on. However, it is an easy trap for any of us to fall into, particularly in the area of problem-solving and advice-giving. Problems are something every prisoner has in abundance: problems of health, wealth, what the family is doing at home, whether he can get a job or parole, whether the letter he expected will come tomorrow, why it hasn't come, whether the nut down the hall will try to rape him again, whether he will die in prison.

It's easy to say that a man must solve his own problems, but sometimes a prisoner cannot solve them, either because being in prison makes solutions impossible, or, as in many cases, because he simply doesn't know how to solve problems. The inmate's problems are real, and not to be taken lightly. However, there is a tendency for the softhearted volunteer to try to carry the burden of the prisoner's problems for him. The only bad thing about this is that the volunteer is not in a position to deal effectively with many of the inmate's problems, and his sleepless nights will not help the prisoner. Furthermore, solutions the volunteer might think effective, and advice he might give, may not be appropriate answers for the prisoner. It is better to satisfy yourself by serving as a resource for the inmate to help him arrive at his own solutions.

One time, a prisoner asked me, "What would you do if . . . ?" and proceeded to tell me about an affair he thought his wife was having with another man. Since my friend was prone to outbursts of temper and violence, and since he was to be released very shortly, the situation shocked me into keeping my mouth shut for a change. I was not sure whether he was seeking advance justification for what he wanted to do to the other man or whether he really didn't know how to solve the problem, but I wasn't willing to take any chances.

We concentrated on the process of problem solving: What was his ultimate objective, the real objective versus the apparent one? What actions or words did he think would help him achieve his aim? Given a series of possible actions toward the goal, what were the potential consequences of each act? I never answered his question, solved his problem, or gave him any advice. Once he understood the problem-solving process, he was able to arrive at his own solutions. And in finding his own answers, he prepared himself to seek alternatives to what might have been a volatile and potentially murderous situation.

In less explosive situations, often the volunteer's tendency is to take on the inmate's burden, giving advice that may not be wanted and offering solutions that may not be workable. But in doing so, you tire yourself and offer poor assistance to the prisoner, who must ultimately accept the problems and responsibility of finding his own solutions.

Another kind of dependence that can hinder the growth of a healthy relationship—if you permit it—is in terms of possessions. Although the prison provides basic necessities, such as food, clothing, and shelter, no prison provides all the things we normally think of as necessities in our society. For example, prisoners must usually provide their own shaving cream and razor blades, facecloths and sometimes facial soap, toothbrush and toothpaste, and a host of other small items. They must certainly provide for themselves nonessential items such as candy, magazines, newspapers, cigarettes, or writing paper.

Prisoners are never permitted to keep money in their possession, although they are permitted to have a "bank account" that is kept for them by the prison. If they have money in their account, they may draw on it to purchase items such as those mentioned above, at the inmate canteen. But since they have no means of acquiring much money in prison, prisoners are totally dependent on the good graces and generosity of family and friends who may put money into their account. In most prisons, if you have befriended someone who has no family or friends to help him, it is permissible for you to put money into his account. Of course, some prisons have strict rules which prohibit you from giving an offender anything, but most institutions do permit at least certain items to be given so long as the package is checked when you enter the prison.

Most men and women in prison are glad to have simply your friendship, respect, and understanding, and if you fulfill an occasional small request or give an unsolicited gift, it is a bonus. Most prisoners will make no demands on you for possessions at all. However, there are some who will have you continually running errands for them—often a sign that you are being badly used. Furthermore, these demands can become a burden, and when the burden is heavy enough, you will weary of it and the relationship you were trying to build will be damaged. A volunteer shouldn't feel guilty about putting the brakes on if an inmate is asking for too much, and the sooner the better in most cases.

A Rule Is to Keep

Mr. Hailey was a relatively new volunteer in a state prison. He was part of a discussion group which met each week and had been coming regularly for several weeks. Following the meeting one evening, as he was on his way toward the main gate, an inmate who was part of his group ran up to him with a request: "Mr. Hailey, I finished this letter too late to get it into the last mail from the prison. It's rather important. Would you mail it on the outside for me?" Well, sure he would mail the letter. Anyone would gladly fulfill such a simple request for a friend.

To Mr. Hailey's surprise, he was detained at the gate by an officer and asked to hand over the letter. What was wrong? The officer pointed to a sign which indicated that the passing of letters was, along with other restrictions, a violation of prison regulations and that violators would be prosecuted. Being a law-abiding person, Mr. Hailey was understandably shaken at the prospect of prosecution. It had never occurred to him that such a simple request could bring the law down on him.

In the end, someone came to his rescue and explained that he had accepted the letter in innocence, and he was not prosecuted; but the prisoner he thought he was helping was sent to the hole. The letter, it turned out, concerned an arrangement for the surreptitious dropoff of a supply of illegal drugs, and the inmate was trying to get past the prison censor. This is known as "kiting" a letter or "sending a kite."

This incident should not be construed as a defense of mail censorship, a policy that still exists in most prisons and which I believe is an unjustifiable invasion of privacy. The point is that since many volunteers agree that rules such as mail censorship are foolish, they tend not to take the rules very seriously. Because they feel a strong sympathy for prisoners who live under these rules, it is easy for them to become partners to violation of them. Such violations occur frequently in prisons and constitute one of the major objections of staff members to volunteers.

I once presented the story of the above incident to a prison officer and asked for his reaction. He said, "Aside from the violation of the law, which is not a very good example to set for an inmate, there is no question that Mr. Hailey was conned by the inmate. The inmate was banking on the man's desire to be friendly and helpful and kind. He was banking on his sympathy for the poor, helpless prisoner. You know, I don't care whether you agree with the rule or not. I don't see how anybody can honestly think he's helping a prisoner by violating the law. Furthermore, I think the volunteer should have been held responsible for knowing the law before he ever entered the prison. Ignorance is no excuse."

Usually, ignorance will not be accepted as an excuse. There should be no question in a volunteer's mind that when asked to violate a prison rule in the name of friendship, he's squarely faced with a level of conning more serious than the types mentioned earlier. It is clear what the volunteer should do: say *no* as firmly as possible. If there is the slightest doubt in your mind whether or not an act is a violation of rules, you can always tell the prisoner, without seeming the least bit unfriendly or unhelpful, that you will be glad to do it if it is permitted, and that you will ask permission.

Such a statement will usually cause an immediate response if the prisoner knows the act is a violation. And this response gives you an opportunity to challenge his motives and his ideas about friendship, which is not an unfair thing for you to do under such circumstances. If the inmate has so little regard for you that he would be willing to lure you into an illegal act for which you could be prosecuted, he does not respect your integrity and he is not your friend. Any volunteer who fears the loss of the prisoner's friendship more than the loss of his own integrity is on an ego trip. The volunteer may or may not get in trouble with the law (depending on whether he is caught), but he certainly is not offering help or friendship to the prisoner.

The myriad of rules, like the time spent in waiting for doors to be locked and unlocked, is one of the frustrations for everyone who resides, works, or volunteers in a prison. Many of the rules are necessary, although the need for them may not be immediately apparent. In addition to the necessary rules, most prisons have an equal number for which no one in his right mind can dream up a reason. Some of them, such as mail censorship, were created long ago and became religiously observed traditions that simply haven't been adequately challenged. Over a long period of time, rules tend to become sacred and people lose sight of the fact that they are nothing more than efficient means to an end. Rules tend to be viewed as ends in themselves long after their usefulness has ended.

In spite of the fact that many rules are more nuisance than help, we can well be more grateful than irritated by a firm set of written rules. The worst kind of prison is the kind that has no set of written rules, because in such places, where rules are arbitrarily created and applied, no inmate is ever quite sure of what he may or may not do. He's never quite certain when the hand of a sadist may descend upon him or whether the door will ever open on freedom again, and if it does, whether he will be physically and psychologically able to walk through it.

Most well-run institutions will either give you a written list of rules or at least explain those that exist. If certain regulations do not make sense to you, question them. However, you would be well advised to pose your questions with great diplomacy. You may attempt to change rules, but to do so you will need the greatest diplomatic skill and ability to maneuver and run around the end of the tackle. You will also need enough experience to find the real sources of power within the institution. Until you develop these skills, it's a good idea to stick to the rules as they are given to you, or you may find yourself on the street.

When you are not too busy sticking to rules, you might contemplate one aspect of prison regulations that inmates are not likely to explain to you. In fact, they may try to do another con job on you by convincing you of how unnecessary all rules are.

A basic set of rules is absolutely essential in any situation— prison or otherwise—in which one person is required to control the behavior and movements of a large group. For example, if there is one child jumping up and down in a living room, we can tolerate the activity even though it might be a nuisance. If, however, there are thirty children doing this in a classroom whenever they feel the urge, the noise level and general chaos will probably be intolerable. Therefore, the teacher makes a rule about jumping up and down. And he sticks to it, or there will be very little learning in the room.

The person controlling the group is also faced with the question about rule-breaking, "What if they all do it?" Whether or not this question is logical really doesn't matter because it hangs in the back of the mind and creates a tendency to "nip things in the bud." If a teacher fails, out of kindness and gentleness, to stop the first bit of horseplay in the classroom, he will soon be taken over by the group and will face horseplay all day long.

The same is true in prison, but since it is a total institution and the inmates live in it twenty-four hours a day, and care a lot less about the place than children do about their school, the opportunities for chaos are far greater than in a school or any other limited institution. Thus, you should not be surprised to find that inmates are frequently punished for what seem to be the most minor kinds of offenses. Officers are required to make reports to the administration regarding prisoners who need to be disciplined, and in these reports are listed a variety of offenses from major ones, such as the possession of weapons, to minor infractions such as swearing at an officer.[1] Some offenses might seem of little import to you, but they are very important to an officer who must maintain his authority and control over what can often be an unruly group of people.

Rules are important to the prison officer or guard because he is charged by both the administration and the public with the tasks of keeping prisoners securely within the prison and maintaining order within the prison, and to do this, he must enforce rules. His problem is to walk a fine line between order and chaos, sensible application of rules and oppressive use of rules. However, this is a very fine line to walk, and if he errs, the tendency is usually to err in the direction of strictness.

You can bet that the role of rule-enforcer doesn't win

officers any popularity among prisoners, and you can be just as sure that many stories you hear about the "screws" and about guard brutality are another feature of the con job. Part of this con job is like the conning I mentioned earlier because it is an unconscious effort by the inmate to make himself look better by painting a bleak picture of those around him. But another part of this game is based on a different attitude. Many inmates tell stories that are simply not true, and officers who are strict will sometimes become known as sadists when, in fact, they aren't. This is unfair to most guards and can damage the relationship between them and volunteers. The officers start to feel that the volunteers look down on them, and they react by not liking volunteers and by making life difficult for them; the volunteers react to this and eventually go away. In the end, the one who is usually hurt by this escalating reaction is the inmate who complained of the mean guards in the first place.

It would be foolish and, indeed, dishonest not to acknowledge that there are sadists among prison officers. There are many incidents of brutality and downright assault which, unfortunately, are rarely prosecuted. As you become acquainted with the prison staff, you will come across bad people who ought to be behind bars themselves. The traditionally low salaries, the absence of training requirements, and the silent remoteness of the prison of the past have often given encouragement to men who could not get other types of work. Some of them, ineffectual in everything else, have found a particular pleasure in exercising absolute and arbitrary control over the lives of prisoners. Officers like this do exist, and they tend to be among those who object most strongly to the presence of volunteers. Your presence cramps their style because they cannot torture inmates when there are witnesses present.

The kinds of torture such guards use may take subtle forms. An officer may humiliate a prisoner by making remarks about a physical or mental deficiency the inmate has. He may make disparaging remarks about an inmate's race or about his wife. He may force a prisoner to do humiliating tasks or refuse permission for the simplest items such as a ration of toilet paper. An officer can continually harass someone he dislikes until the inmate finally strikes out in a rage. The moment a prisoner lifts a hand toward a guard, he is subject to several possible consequences: an immediate beating which can easily be covered up as self-defense by the guard, being sent to the hole, loss of visits or mail, loss of good time, or a new criminal charge for the attempted assault of a correctional officer.

Such incidents can and do happen in any completely closed institution, and the only way to prevent them is to keep the prison constantly open to outside scrutiny. This means open primarily to volunteers, and it means that volunteers must get along with staff, the majority of whom do not fit the above description.

There are several ways to get along with prison officers, and they are not difficult. The first, of course, is obvious: obey orders and rules without grumbling. Officers aren't accustomed to having anyone argue with them over the merits of regulations, and they tend to have a dim view of people who act as though they are lawyers defending the constitution. As one guard put it, "Look. I didn't make the rule. I just enforce it. And if you don't like it, go see your congressman or go see the boss, but don't argue with me."

The second way of getting along with officers is far better. If you have a bleeding heart—and you know you do—try to spare a few drops for the guards, as well as the prisoners. They have a very difficult job to do, and they live with the stone walls and iron bars all day or all night just as the prisoners do; they suffer some of the same frustrations of institutional life. Even if all your sentiments are with the prisoners, the very least you owe the officers is an open mind. And if sentiment is lacking, you can offer them the respect they need to function well; they need respect as much as the inmates need it or anyone else needs it. And when you hear stories about the guards, you can at least give them the same benefit of the doubt you would give a prisoner. It isn't necessary to say or do anything to communicate attitudes, and if you communicate a reasonably good attitude toward officers, you will usually receive reasonably good responses.

Prisoners feel a certain resentment for all officers, and they give them a certain amount of resistance, simply because officers automatically represent the authority structure which is keeping them behind bars. Yet, a thorough examination of any prison will show quite clearly that, all stories to the contrary, prisoners and guards are not usually in the state of warfare that many people imagine. Even the toughest people could not exist very long under such a condition. Indeed, because of backgrounds that have accustomed most prisoners to hardship, their survival has depended at least in part on toughness, and it is one thing they respect. Translated, this means that most inmates respect an officer who does his job well, who is fair and strict. They do not respect an officer who can be manipulated any more than they respect a volunteer who can be easily conned.

I know one officer who is the exact antithesis of what most readers would consider a civilized gentleman. He is crude, poorly educated, unmannerly, openly bigoted against a variety of groups (particularly eggheads), unpleasant in countenance, and among the most profane individuals imaginable. It is not at all difficult for me to imagine him in situations in which he is the leading character performing dastardly acts. I am afraid of him, and I cannot view him as a person doing what some of us like to think ought to be a professional job; but he is very effective. Because he is one of the most frequently cursed-out guards, I first thought he was effective because he was cruel. In fact, I discovered, he is effective because he fulfills the inmates' vision of a tough guy who can't be fooled. Although he is crude, he knows how to make the men laugh. He sees through every little con job, and knows how to head off trouble before it starts. He knows exactly who is doing what to whom and can correct situations without giving inmates the feeling they are being persecuted. Since he is not arrogant, he is quite capable of overlooking the little improprieties that would cause a more idealistic officer to retaliate. It appears, indeed, that underneath all his gruffness and profanity, he's soft as a grape. He is also one of the most popular officers in the prison.

When they are pressed, most inmates will admit there are many good officers in their prison. In most cases, the good ones are a majority. Both prisoners and officers can tell a number of stories about good relations between them. And, on occasion, inmates will even tell about guards who gave them assistance that went far beyond the call of duty. Of course, this spirit sometimes flows in two directions. Many readers will recall that several inmates who participated in the bloody revolt at Attica in 1971 died from the troopers' bullets after having used their own bodies as shields for their officer-hostages. No act could portray more dramatically that their grievances were far less against the officers than against the system itself.

Yet, the decency of the many good officers tends to be lost in the midst of hysteria—in the process of trying to locate a suitable scapegoat for the problems of prisons. As a group, officers rightly resent being viewed as the bad guys, especially by volunteers who come into the prison, do the good-guy jobs, go home, and leave the tough jobs for someone else. The officers deserve better than that.

Most of the con jobs you will encounter in prison are similar to the ones I've discussed. But now and then, you should be prepared to meet the professional con artist. He is a man who, from an early time in his life, has learned to make deception the means of his existence. He may not necessarily intend to deceive you, but it is an ingrained habit that he doesn't know how to stop. He may have started by becoming an artist at convincing his mother he didn't get mud on his pants—someone threw it on him—because failure to convince her may have meant a beating. He may have led teachers into believing it was not he who threw the paper airplane—no, he wouldn't do that, and risk going to the principal. On several occasions, judges may have been moved by his tears, which he learned to turn on at a moment's notice, or by his promises never to steal again in his whole life. Lying became a matter of survival, and now that he is grown up, he is in the business of deception for profit.

Neil was just such a professional con artist. He was young, handsome, intelligent, articulate, and sophisticated—one of the most charming men one could wish to meet and talk with. It wouldn't have been difficult to imagine him as an Ivy League Ph.D. candidate who somehow got into prison by a terrible mistake.[2] But Neil's fabrications had got him in trouble, so he decided he needed psychiatric care, and it was arranged for him upon his release.

Neil never failed to appear for the sessions with his psychiatrist. On one occasion, after they had known one another for a while, he was telling the doctor about his pleasures and problems in a new business venture. The doctor was interested and shared what he knew about business, and Neil was grateful and thanked him as he left. He continued to give the doctor detailed reports on his business with each visit, and it sounded as though things were going very well.

One day, however, he was rather glum and admitted that because of a customer who was forced to be late in payments, he was in a difficult financial spot. He knew the customer would pay eventually, but in the meantime he didn't know how to meet his commitments. He feared that his prison record would surface, and it would be the end of everything for him. What did he need to bail him out? A loan of $10,000.

The doctor gave Neil the loan and has not seen him since. When he began to investigate, he discovered that the business his patient had been describing in such minute detail had never existed and that, indeed, he had swindled three other people out of $10,000 each. The only nice thing that can be said about Neil is that he had the decency to swindle four people who could afford it, and in the process he may have taught the psychiatrist and his other victims something they didn't know about deviant behavior. Unfortunately, $40,000 is an expensive price for such a lesson.

I'm not at all sure about how to prevent volunteers from falling into the big or little pitfalls of prison life. I am told that a criminology professor, bent on preparing his students properly, brought to class an elderly, professional con artist whom he had known during his years of prison work. Anton had reformed a little by then because of old age and the inability to keep up with the hustle, and this venerable gentleman, which he certainly appeared to be, explained to the students the precise techniques he used to soften up his victims. The students roared with laughter, wondering how anyone could be stupid enough to fall for it. The lecture was a fantastic success, and everyone wanted to know Anton a little better. Not until some time later did the professor discover that Anton had done in several of his brilliant students. Only small amounts of money were involved, to be sure, for Anton had developed a conscience. But those amounts were gone forever. Perhaps one truly learns only by experience!

The Meaning of Success

One of the ways to protect yourself from con artists is to be honest about the differences between you and your friend in prison. The main distinction between the majority of volunteers and most prison inmates is social background, and since one's experiences in early life influence him forever, what I am saying is that the differences between you and prisoners are likely to be immense. These varieties of experience present each person with a different set of opportunities and values, and ways of seeing the world.

It is fairly likely that most readers will fall into the profile of today's prison volunteer I described in the preceding chapter. That is, you may be among the white, middle-class or upper-middle-class people who have the training, comfort, leisure, and social conscience to concern yourselves with a less fortunate group. You're probably successful in the world's eyes and believe the means to success can be taught to others.

I think all of us occasionally succumb to the notion that the way we do things is the right way; after all, it worked for us. Those of us who have achieved what the world considers to be success think we have the key to the method. And some of us make a religion of our theories—believing that nothing but good can come from our proselytizing.

The trouble with this attitude, whether one tries to teach the method of material success or moral goodness, is that it may not work for your friend in prison. When their theories haven't worked, many volunteers have thrown up their hands in despair and quit. They either quit entirely or stop working with the offender who, a few months earlier, was very important to them. There is great spiritual pain for the volunteer who does not control his expectations, and perhaps even worse pain for the offender because he then feels an additional failure that reinforces his low estimate of his capabilities. This is the last thing in the world he needs.

Thus one must be careful about the concept of success. Like many other concepts, the idea of success is relative and depends on your vantage point, upbringing, social class, education, and luck. And the experiences of most prison inmates have been quite different from yours. You should not expect your friend in prison to become the president of the second national bank or even to consider such a position as an aim. Earning a decent income and keeping out of prison again might be his notion of success. You should anticipate a level of success for your friend, but the goal should always be related to his starting position, for we all advance by degrees and not by magic.

Related to the notion of worldly success is the idea of success as the ability to stay out of prison entirely. Many volunteers make a great emotional investment in the prisoners they befriend, and this is good. However, because of this investment, they may be quite shattered if their friends reappear in prison for a new crime. After several years of working in prisons, I still have not overcome the sinking feeling that occurs when an inmate I've worked with comes back to prison, and anyone who works with offenders over a period of time is certain to encounter this situation. You'll never feel good about it, but you can learn to take it in stride so that you aren't deeply hurt.

Recidivism is always depressing for both the offender and the volunteer, but it helps both of you if you can put it in perspective. Are you going to hurt your friend by rejecting him for what you consider to be a failure, a lack of success in your eyes? Or is it a total failure? Perhaps it is only a temporary setback, but you are disappointed because your emotional investment has not paid off as well as you had expected. Perhaps you are angry with the inmate, not because he hurt himself or someone else, but because he hurt you and your expectations. Like disappointment in an offender's material success, the sadness you feel when an ex-inmate returns to prison can also be limited by keeping goals in realistic relationship to the inmate's starting point.

Imagine what would have happened if our parents had given up on us after our first clumsy attempts to tie a shoelace. We have to think in terms of improvement rather than perfection.

Consider these two instances. A young woman of twenty-six had been a prostitute since she was sixteen, and over a period of years became hooked on heroin and subsequently went to prison for a drug offense. While in prison, she was forced to give up heroin, and later agreed that giving it up was a good idea. Her habit had reduced her to a near vegetable, and she had spent all her time and effort getting money to support it; she had nothing else left in life. In prison she took a secretarial course to help her get started in a new career and met a volunteer who gave her a great deal of emotional support and helped her when she got out. On leaving prison, she entered a methadone program, stayed off heroin, and got a nice, if not very profitable, job. It seemed as though she had really "gotten it together."

When she later appeared in prison again, her volunteer friend was very discouraged, and jumped to the immediate conclusion, "What made you go back to the stuff?"

"Oh, I haven't," said the woman. "I wouldn't spend my money on that stuff any more. I've been doing better without it. Got a nice apartment, good clothes, a lot of things I never had before. I've got a decent life now. I just got picked up for tricking this time, but it's only a short stretch."

I don't know why the volunteer was so surprised that the woman had returned to prostitution, a profession that was familiar to her and was considerably more profitable than working as a typist. For some people, prostitution on any scale may seem repugnant, but to her it was a way of life and could not be considered a failure. Also, she was successful in that she was using all her profits for the things she really wanted rather than for heroin. The general state of her life has to be seen as an improvement on what it was when she was using heroin, in spite of the fact that she continued in behavior that is illegal.

The second case involved a man I knew. He had been convicted of one armed robbery, but we all knew he had conducted a number of robberies before he was caught and endangered many lives by his use of weapons. After he served his term, he was out for about five years before he was caught again; this time he had stolen a car, but there were no weapons involved.

Some people may judge this second incarceration as a sign of failure, but I don't think it is. Considering his history of crime since youth—an ingrained pattern—and the ease with which he could have obtained a gun if he had wanted one, this last crime is a clear advance from his violent past. Though he was still engaged in crime, he had gradually become only a nuisance rather than a threat to anyone's personal safety. Thus, his second incarceration must be considered a setback rather than a total failure.

In short, it is necessary to expect and demand some level of success for your friend in prison, or he won't achieve anything. But, to save yourself a lot of heartache, you should be clear about what "success" means for a particular individual. You've got to build him up by leaving certain of his deceptions unchallenged, but you have to be sensitive about how far his deception can go. You have to expect some change in his behavior, but you need to be sure your demands are based on his experiences rather than yours. You need to protect yourself by realizing that when you step into an area of work that tries to change human behavior—yours, his, or anyone's—you have stepped into an uncharted land for which no one has a compass.

5

WOMEN
ON TRIAL

"Long live male chauvinism" might well be the motto of any woman who falls on the wrong side of the law. Of all the thousands of people in prison today, only 4 to 5 percent are women, and in view of the fact that we represent approximately one-half the population, that's not a bad record at all. Part of that record, I suspect, is due to the very male chauvinism we rail against.

Consider the fact that the offender's first contact with the criminal justice system is through a policeman. And if you observe or question a broad selection of policemen, you will find that the majority of them still subscribe to a kind of chivalric view of women as the fair sex who should be pursued in romance rather than in a police car. Most of them view women as sweet, fragile things who are desperately in need of their masculine strength and protection. So, for the most part, a policeman's tendency is to treat women as he treats juveniles: lecturing them sternly or giving them tickets, but rarely subjecting them to the condemnatory process of going to jail, or even to court. There is a general hesitancy to arrest a woman unless she is a persistent nuisance or has committed a crime of sufficient seriousness that it cannot be overlooked.

If a woman is foolish enough to overstep the line of discretion, of course, she may be arrested and taken to court. Once in court she will meet a judge who might be more sophisticated in his manner of expression than the policeman, but he shares the policeman's attitude of chivalry toward her. He doesn't like to send women to prison. Thus, unless she has committed murder or mayhem, or her immoral behavior has become a thorough nuisance to the community, she can usually get off with either a fine or probation. Even if she is a persistent repeater of minor crimes, she will usually be granted fines or probation many more times than a man would be before he was sent to prison.

A scene I watched in court one day is typical of the differences in treatment accorded the sexes: A woman of about thirty appeared before the judge on a charge of possession of heroin. The arresting officers had done quite a thorough job, and the evidence was so heavily stacked against her that her lawyer did not even challenge it. The situation looked pretty grim for her, especially when it was revealed that this was her eighth conviction for a series of crimes involving drugs, larceny, petty larceny, drunkenness, and shoplifting. She had never been sentenced to prison, and I thought to myself, "They'll throw the book at her this time." After all the facts were heard, the woman stood, quiet and submissive, the picture of remorse and penitence, as the group of men gathered around the judge decided her fate in whispers. The verdict? Guilty, of course. Five years' probation.

"Next case!" shouted the court officer. Two young men in their early twenties had just been apprehended and were accused of assault with a dangerous weapon and intent to rob. Both had one previous conviction for larceny, and both were unemployed, unkempt, hostile-looking men. They asked for a continuance so they could get a lawyer. The continuance was granted, but a bail of $2,000 each was set, which neither of them could meet. So, off to jail they went.

There is little doubt that the judge's paternalism helped keep the woman out of prison. Obviously, he and all the other men involved treated her more like an errant child than a criminal. But there was more to their judgment than favoritism. The reader will note that although this woman had a long record of offenses, there was no record of a weapon or any form of violence in her history. In that sense, she was typical of most female offenders. Many women are arrested on morals charges, such as prostitution, vagrancy, alcoholism, or drug addiction, and many more are convicted of property thefts, such as petty larceny, larceny, passing bad checks, and shoplifting. Women have by no means cornered the market on virtue, but they are, as a group, more civilized and less violent than men. Very few women carry a gun or any kind of dangerous weapon, and while crimes in which women use weapons have increased in recent years, most female offenders are simply not regarded as being dangerous to other people. Because of the weapon involved the two young men were regarded as a threat to the community, but society was in little peril from the woman, in spite of her seven previous convictions. Women's harm to themselves is greater than their harm to others.

If the double standard appears to favor women prior to conviction, it certainly does not work in their favor when they are sentenced to jail or prison. Indeed, prison seems in some ways to have harsher consequences for women than for men.

The first of these consequences results from a labeling process. The nursery rhyme that ends "And when she was good, she was very very good, but when she was bad, she was horrid" is symbolic of our traditional views about women. Our society expects women to be soft, gentle, innocent, virginal, and noncriminal. We have consistently put woman on a pedestal, so that when she falls from that precarious height, like a plaster statue, she is broken into pieces. Her reputation is shattered, and society generally perceives her as evil or worthless.

A woman's crime very often seems more reprehensible than a man's because it is so far removed from our image of womanly behavior. A murder is a murder no matter who commits it or by what means. But Lady Macbeth's plan to murder Duncan strikes terror in the soul because one does not expect a woman to have the harshness or insensitivity for such a deed. No one likes to see a drunk lying in the gutter, but somehow it seems more loathsome if the drunk is a woman because our image of womanly dignity is assaulted. We don't openly approve of a young man who is sexually promiscuous, but we forgive him and excuse him with "he's just sowing his wild oats." But despite the advent of the birth-control pill and sexual "liberation," promiscuity isn't approved for young women. The girl who behaves in this fashion is condemned and labeled as surely as Hester was by her famous "A."

A certain amount of youthful foolishness and even danger-ous exuberance are almost expected of a young man, but such behavior is not expected or easily forgiven in women. Since the police and courts are generally more lenient with women in the first place, a woman's presence in prison is usually thought to mean that she is truly incorrigible. The label of delinquent or criminal is more damaging to women than men; even delinquent boys—the rough toughs of the streets—want little to do with the girl who carries the same label. Many women never manage to overcome the stigma of these labels, and sink further and fur-ther into hopelessness.

Prison seems to be harder on women than men for a second reason: it has harmful effects on her image of herself as a woman. Some people think that a woman has two socially ac-ceptable roles in life, her relationships with men and her rela-tionships with children. This is not necessarily how things ought to be, but it is how they are. If this idea is true, and I think to a large extent it is, a woman finds it very difficult to maintain her image as a woman while in prison, since she is stripped of all relations with men and children. A man in prison can preserve a certain sense of manliness by simply acting tough and perverse and by obeying the inmate code of solidarity, but this sort of be-havior is useless in trying to maintain femininity.

Instead, women in prison create the temporary family struc-tures and affectionate roles they so sorely miss. Some play mother, daughter, or wife; others play the male roles of husband, father, or lover. This role-playing fosters a much higher degree of homosexuality than is generally found in male prisons. Although most women return to heterosexual patterns when they are re-leased from prison, the homosexual experiences cause them psy-chological problems they could do without.[1]

Prison is more harmful to women than to men for yet an-other reason: because of what it does to their children. When men go to prison, they usually assume that their wives, or some woman, will take care of their children, even if it has to be done under the very straitened circumstances of a welfare budget. But the woman who goes to prison can make no such assumption. In most cases, her children become wards of the state and are placed in foster homes. Often they are shifted from one home to another, growing up in a cycle of neglect, insecurity, and potential delinquency. Many women in prison don't know a faithful man they can depend on to care for their children, and some weren't decent mothers in the first place. But whatever the circumstances, women worry about their children when they are absent from them. For women in prison, this worry turns to nightmare as they wonder about their children's welfare and whereabouts and feel remorse for having failed them.

The dual standard further handicaps a woman when she is being released from prison. Like the male ex-inmate, the woman was usually poor before she went to prison, but even if she wasn't poor before, she certainly is by the time she gets out. When you are very poor, the problem of acquiring a place to live at a price you can afford (which is almost nothing) is acute. In many cases it is almost impossible for female ex-inmates to find a place to live unless they have good jobs with decent pay, which they usually don't. If finding a good job is difficult for a male ex-inmate—and it is—his problem is minuscule compared to the difficulty a female ex-inmate has. In our society, good, responsible jobs with salaries adequate to support a family are hard for any woman to get, even if she is a well-educated, well-trained, mature woman with a record as a hard worker and has never had a traffic ticket. But if a woman has an erratic work record, or none at all, a medium to poor education, and a prison record, the outlook is grim. Thus, the average female ex-inmate faces a hostile community, children to support and no spouse to help her with them, no place to live, no decent job, and (for about 50 percent) an addiction to drugs or an alcohol problem. It should come as no surprise that a high percentage of female ex-inmates get in trouble with the law on a regular basis.

Perhaps because female prisoners are such a small percentage of the total prison population, they have received short shrift from social scientists and from the public at large. But they need understanding, help, and attention every bit as much as men.

The volunteer will find women prisoners in two main settings and kinds of conditions.

Women in Jail

Since most female offenders are convicted of relatively minor crimes which carry short prison sentences, most of them are sentenced to local city or county jails. There are over 4,000 city and county jails in the country, and conditions vary considerably from place to place, but it is safe to say that no matter what state you live in, the conditions in the local jails are almost always worse than in large state or federal prisons.

A few large cities, such as New York, have enough female prisoners to warrant a facility totally separate from the male prisoners. In most places, however, women prisoners are kept in a separate wing of the same building that houses men. In some places, like Houston, women don't even have individual cells but are kept in what are called tanks. And in cities and counties such as Boston, Westchester, Washington, Chicago, and Milwaukee—in towns all across the country—the lot of women in jail is the same. They mop the floors, polish the steps, and clean the administrative offices of the jail. In some jails they do the laundry or sew uniforms for the whole institution. And in other jails they do nothing—nothing but vegetate.

What can the volunteer do? Everything. Since most women in jail have nothing—no possessions, no place to go, nothing to do, no officially sponsored programs—almost any volunteer-sponsored program is an improvement on existing conditions. If you are itching for a sense of accomplishment and want to see things happen, the place to work is with women prisoners. It is one of the terrible ironies of our correctional system that in jails, where we keep people who are awaiting trial and those convicted of the smallest offenses, we permit the worst physical and psychological conditions found in any part of the prison system.

Since jail prisoners are usually incarcerated for short periods of time, voluntary programs should be geared to activities that can be accomplished in a period of six to ten weeks. Also, programs in jails have to be very flexible since they serve a continually changing population. In addition, the characteristics of the inmates will vary considerably in different parts of the country, or even in different counties within the same state. For example, in one area you may find that many of the women in jail are destitute alcoholics; in another they may be mostly prostitutes; and in a large city jail they will be a mixture of many kinds of people.

In order to create a meaningful program for women in a jail, you need a number of volunteers who can survey the population of the jail and find out what activities most of the women need and want. What they want is very important because no matter how much you think they need a certain kind of help, it will be useless unless the women want it. You also need volunteers who can provide a variety of activities that can be altered according to changing needs.

The Citizens' Committee of Westchester County, New York, organized an excellent volunteer program for short-term offenders, and in 1971 they prepared a valuable detailed, written account of how they developed a program for women (available from the National Council on Crime and Delinquency). Their initial survey indicated that the women were most interested in creative activities such as handcrafts, sewing, personal grooming, child care, music, writing, and painting. So the volunteers began to offer courses in these areas. Education was also needed, since many of the women, though literate, had not finished high school. Courses were then started in English, mathematics, science, and social studies, all leading to a high school diploma.

Jail inmates awaiting trial are frequently not around long enough to participate in courses such as those listed above, particularly the educational courses. Also, people awaiting trial are usually in a state of extreme tension and uncertainty about what is going to happen to them. Because of the emotional stress, it is very difficult for them to concentrate on academic courses. However, they universally claim they "need something to do," something to occupy the time and absorb some of their frustration. And they generally prefer a creative activity.

Many women in jail occupy themselves with knitting or crocheting, if someone provides the materials for them. There is nothing wrong with this, except that it is very limited in scope. Other activities can easily be introduced if there are volunteers who will spend time teaching other arts. Some people can do this almost single-handedly.

One such person is Maggie Sherwood, a New York photographer who operates a houseboat called the Floating Foundation of Photography. Some time ago, she sponsored courses in photography at New York State prisons for men. Then she began a course for women at the Women's House of Detention in New York City. The women not only love it, but have produced some excellent photographic works under extremely difficult limitations.

A group in the Cook County Jail in Chicago conducts a charm school under the sponsorship of the Clement Stone Foundation. This, too, is very popular with women prisoners and has now been introduced in ten other jails. Its basic purpose, in addition to filling time, is to help women build up their self-image. Thus, the activity fills a more significant need than one would imagine on first hearing the words *charm school*.

There is no reason that a host of similar activities shouldn't be available in every jail. However, all these activities should be regarded as stopgap measures. While they make life a little more bearable for women in jail, they do not and cannot get to the real problems of these women. Women in jail or prison have a multitude of personal and social problems which the criminal justice system is ill equipped to deal with. In fact, it exacerbates their problems. I think the effects of incarceration are so serious and permanent that an offender's danger to other people should be the only cause for such harsh action. Since very few women have proven themselves dangerous to anyone but themselves, the best thing we could do for most incarcerated women is get them out of jail as quickly as possible.

This means that the most significant assistance you can give women prisoners is in two areas. First of all, they need legal assistance. There is a growing number of female lawyers who are relatively well organized as a group. A great deal of their attention is currently directed to the battle for women's rights, which is good. However, it would also be good for these groups to spend more time assisting women in jail, most of whom are indigent or close to it and can't afford good lawyers. I don't mean to exempt male lawyers from responsibility, but they have been around for a long time and have shown little interest in assisting women prisoners. It may be up to other women to help them.

The second important need of female prisoners is for laws to be changed. Most incarcerated women are in jail for the victimless crimes of prostitution, alcoholism, and drug addiction. So long as imprisonment is permitted as a penalty for these offenses, women will continue to go to jail and prison. In particular, laws prohibiting prostitution militate against women, and a high percentage of female prisoners have been involved in it, some as a profession and many as a means of supporting a drug habit. "In 1968, in the District of Columbia, 112 men were prosecuted for patronage of prostitution; there were 8,000 prosecutions of women for soliciting." [2] Women don't solicit unless there are customers, so the inequity is obvious. I don't suggest that we should necessarily legalize or encourage prostitution, but we should limit legal penalties to fines rather than incarceration. And we should have community centers for those women who need and want help in changing their pattern of life. They don't need jail.

The Female Felon

Of course, not all female offenders are lucky enough to get probation or short jail sentences. Some women are persistent offenders, and others have committed serious crimes. Several thousand women in this category can be found in state penitentiaries or reformatories for women.

Both the federal prison system and more than half the state systems have separate prisons for women. Although they are nobody's idea of a nice place to stay, most of them have better conditions than those provided for male prisoners. Part of the reason is that most administrators of women's prisons have looked to Alderson, the federal prison for women in West Virginia, as a model; most professionals have considered it to be the best prison in the country for women, at least in terms of humane treatment. In the last few years, women at Alderson have been permitted to wear their own clothes rather than prison garb, and have been able to set up their own work programs. They have an educational program and some vocational training, and there is counseling. Also, the prison has an enlightened warden. This doesn't sound like much, perhaps, but it is a clear advance over what women had in the old days, perhaps ten years ago, when conditions in women's prisons closely paralleled those still existing in most jails.

Many state reformatories are also modeled on Alderson in terms of their physical plants. A number are built on the "cottage plan," which means there might be from ten to eighty women in a series of houses on the grounds. The women usually have individual rooms rather than the barred cells found in male prisons, and they often have some freedom to decorate their rooms as they want. The setting may look more like a college campus than a prison and be surrounded only by a fence rather than the foreboding stone walls of traditional prisons. In general, prisons for women have far less crowding, fewer security restrictions, and allow inmates much more freedom of movement than male institutions. However, the fact that some women's prisons have better physical conditions than male prisons doesn't mean these institutions are any less problematical for the women in them.

First of all, like male prisons, most female prisons are situated in rural areas and are difficult to travel to. For example, Alderson, which houses women from all over the country, is a five- to six-hour drive from Washington, D.C., and the nearest national airport. Imagine what a journey it is for a visitor coming from New York or San Francisco. Though state institutions aren't quite so remotely located, their distance from populated areas is always considerable, and this discourages visits from friends and relatives. The prisoner thus faces a loneliness and consequent despair that is hard to endure. Also, the lovely countryside is not always appreciated by the majority of inmates, who are from urban areas. Most women at Alderson no doubt view the surrounding mountains more as a natural wall blocking their freedom than as a glorious natural phenomenon.

The superior physical conditions in women's prisons shouldn't blind us into thinking that female inmates have fewer personal problems than men or need assistance any less. One of the few extensive studies prepared on female offenders was done at the California Institution for Women in Frontera, California.[3] Frontera is the largest institution for women in the country, and it is probably safe to say that the population there isn't very different from that of other women's prisons. Seventy-eight percent of the women at Frontera were imprisoned either for property crimes or narcotics offenses. Eighty-nine percent of the women had had previous trouble with the law and had been arrested, fined, on probation, or served earlier prison sentences. Most of the previous charges against them had involved narcotics and/or prostitution.

In short, most of them are women who have had a history of trouble with the law. It is interesting to note, however, that their previous trouble with the law was usually for the same victimless crimes—narcotics, alcohol, and prostitution—that we find among women serving short sentences in county jails and houses of correction. Some of the women at Frontera were in the state prison, serving long sentences because of serious crimes such as murder. But many of them graduated to the state prison simply because society—represented by a judge, in this case—became tired of their petty crimes and decided to "teach them a lesson." It's a pretty tough and strange sort of lesson.

The women in penitentiaries share with male prison populations many deficiencies in educational and vocational training, along with the criminal stigma that does so much damage to them and their future. They have a lot of lesson-learning to do if they are to stay out of trouble in the future. And what do we do for these women? Even at Alderson, long considered the model prison for women, the major work program is in a garment factory that makes uniforms for federal men's prisons. This situation is typical of most women's prisons. Some institutions even have the effrontery to try to convince the public that "learning the garment industry" is a significant vocational education program. A few other classic favorites are "learning the culinary arts," which, translated, means the women work in the prison kitchen; "studying laundry operation," which means they do the wash for the institution; and "studying horticulture," which means they work on a farm. These training programs are akin to the manufacturing of license plates in men's prisons; not quite so useless, but almost, since very few of the women will pursue these arts as future careers.

Of course, there are other, more modern vocational training programs as well. Frontera is proud of its key-punch operator's course, the Illinois Reformatory considers its cosmetology course among the best, and the Florida Correctional Institution offers a good nurse's-aide training program. These are becoming more and more typical, as are the secretarial-training programs found in many institutions. Programs in some women's institutions are very good and others are only token activities.

But consider two important facts. Many women in prison have narcotics addictions that are very expensive to maintain. So far, no alternative, methadone included, has had a high success rate in getting people off serious drug habits. Secondly, many of these same women, as well as others who aren't addicts, have been involved in the high-paying business of prostitution. We don't have means for successfully competing with these life-styles.

I don't suggest we should forget educational or vocational programs that provide alternatives. But I do think we ought to be realistic in our expectations of how much they can achieve with most female inmates. We shouldn't expect the prison to work miracles that the wider society hasn't been able to bring about. How can work in the "garment industry," the "culinary arts," or even a job as a nurse's aide compete with the financial rewards of prostitution?

In addition to the job problem, there is often the question of an entire life-style. Should we expect a young woman who was living high before prison, swinging, to settle down to the humdrum existence of a typing pool or a laundry operation when she gets out? My guess is that to expect such a change to occur before the woman is thirty or thirty-five is unrealistic. Certainly, her experience in prison isn't going to hasten the change, and it may well retard it.

Women who are released from penitentiaries face the same problems in acquiring jobs as women or men coming out of jails. And the longer they are incarcerated, the more difficult is the adjustment. Licensing boards hesitate to grant licenses—as nurse's aides, for example—to those who aren't considered of good moral character. A woman has the same problem as a man in getting even a driver's license. She faces the same hesitancy by employers to hire an ex-con.

It's not a pretty picture in any case, and it is worse if the woman has a child. A woman who has been incarcerated for a long period of time often has trouble regaining custody of her child, since the child has been a ward of the state. If there was a close relative willing to take custody while the mother was in prison, the relative may have kept in contact with her, and she may be reunited with the child without much difficulty. If the child was placed in a foster home and the foster parents were diligent about maintaining contact, the relationship may still be intact. But if the child was placed with irresponsible foster parents, or was shifted to several homes, contact may have been lost. The child may not want to join the mother after a long and resented separation, or the foster parents may not want to give up custody. The child-welfare agency, which now has official custody of the child in the name of the state, can say, "Sorry, you cannot have your child until you have a permanent home to keep him in and a permanent job by which to support him." The mother may have neither a home nor a job for quite a while after she is released.

The caseworker in charge of the child has an inordinate amount of power, in most states, in making decisions about whether, and when, the mother is capable of caring for her child. The only recourse for the woman is in the courts, a path most newly released women are ill prepared to pursue either financially or emotionally. As a result, the mother often has a fierce emotional battle with the child, the foster parents, or the child-welfare agency. In the end, both mother and child are badly scarred.

In addition to job, housing, and child problems, the female ex-inmate faces the difficulty of a strongly disapproving community. Can she get the community acceptance without which her other problems aren't likely to be resolved? People usually fear women ex-cons almost as much as male ex-inmates, and because they often expect the worst, that's what they sometimes get. It's a little hypocritical to speak of accepting female ex-inmates "when they get out." Acceptance of them as people must begin while the women are still on the inside, which means there must be a massive input of community members—volunteers—into prisons for as long as there are prisons.

Edna L. Goodrich, Superintendent of the relatively new Purdy Treatment Center for Women in Washington State, recognized the necessity for volunteers in women's prisons and encouraged the most extensive volunteer program I've seen in a female prison. There may be similar programs I haven't heard about, but this one can serve as a model. The volunteer program at Purdy includes every type of activity mentioned in chapter 2, so that every kind of talent in the community can be used in the institution. The activities include a one-to-one sponsorship (a W-2 Program patterned on the M-2 Program for men), library assistance, a recreation program, music, arts, crafts, and assistance in vocational training. The community is involved in every aspect of the prison, and the program is permeated with the basic aim of bringing the offender and the community together again. If you operate a wide variety of activities under this philosophical umbrella, it's bound to have an impact.

The problems of the female offender are no less worrisome at Purdy than elsewhere and are no less difficult to cope with. But this program is more productive and increases the women's chances for success more than any other program I've seen. It is one example of a community working for the progress of all its members, and that's what volunteer programs in any state prison should be about. They should be concerned with absorbing women prisoners into the community so the institution becomes unnecessary.

THE PLIGHT OF
THE CHILDREN

"Now I'll know he ain't in trouble," she sighed with some relief. Jimmie's mother didn't defend him and didn't resist or object to the judge's decision that Jimmie spend the next six months at the state training school. She was weary after the day in court, tired and weary. Without a tear or the slightest emotional expression, she and Jimmie parted; he with his head hanging and she whispering, "You behave yourself now, hear? I'll be out to see you." Jimmie was someone else's headache now.

Jimmie is twelve years old now—a big boy for his age—and he's been trouble to people for several years. He first appeared in court when he was eleven because he wasn't going to school. But he didn't just disappear on a fine spring day to go fishing; he absconded first for days at a time, then for weeks. With so much time on his hands, it wasn't long before he began to get into petty mischief, stealing candies and fruit from local merchants. Then he managed to shoplift some fancy clothes from a department store. Stealing became an exciting and profitable pastime for him.

Jimmie's mother was at her wit's end. Jimmie was the third of five children; his father had deserted them years earlier, and she had worked hard to keep a roof over their heads. Life had been hard for her, and she was easily irritated after a long day; she had no time or energy for more problems. She could barely cope with existence, and clearly could not cope with Jimmie, who grew more sassy each day.

Jimmie needed special attention. At

the time of his first court appearance, he was technically in the fifth grade, although he looked older because of his size. However, he could read only on a third grade level and had been pushed on from grade to grade in school because of his size. He was never fond of school, but as time passed, everything there made him miserable. He couldn't do the work, couldn't keep up, and wouldn't ask for special help, which he shouldn't have had to ask for anyway. Instead, he cut up, and finally cut·out.

At first Jimmie was put on probation and a student probation aide tutored him. The young tutor liked Jimmie, took him to a few ball games, let him tag along at many of his own activities, and generally took a strong brotherly interest in him. Jimmie loved this attention, and began doing quite well under the tutorship. He even appeared in school again, attendance being one of the aims of his probation.

Then came the teachers' strike, and Jimmie was on the street again for weeks in a row. Although he continued his lessons with his tutor, and the tutor gave him as much time as he could, it wasn't enough. The temptations of the street were too much, and one day, taunted by a few other boys about a suspiciously new shirt he was wearing, Jimmie lashed out, into a roaring brawl. His opponent landed in the hospital with a broken arm and several stitches on his face. Jimmie's record now read: persistent truancy, petty theft, assault and battery, and the means of correction was the State Training School for Boys.

"Aw, don't feel so bad," said a young tough as he gave Jimmie an encouraging back slap. "The place I came from was so bad they tore it down to build a slum." Jimmie giggled in spite of himself. The boys had been making the usual inquiries about a new mate: where he came from, what he had done, how tough he was.

Jimmie had stood out in his old school, a little because of his size, but more because his educational problems were worse than those of the others in his class. His behavior in school was more disruptive, his family had more problems, and he had a bad reputation because he had been through court. He was the kind of boy parents told their children to keep away from. "He's a bad influence," they said.

But at the training school, Jimmie wasn't the least bit unusual; all the boys there have similar problems. A look through the records at their case histories is like playing with a beanbag —you can poke it here and there to make slightly different shapes, but in the end it's the same beanbag.

Most of the boys in Jimmie's group come from homes that have been broken by either death, divorce, or desertion (the three *D*'s of the juvenile business). Some have been physically abused by one of their parents or by relatives who substituted as part-time parents. Others have been neglected by parents who are either mentally incompetent or are emotional children themselves and too disturbed to comprehend the damage they do to their children. A few of the parents are well known to the juvenile court because they appeared there themselves a decade earlier.

All the boys at the training school are in trouble, and they are boys who have a lot of troubles. They are the children nobody wants, whom few adults know what to do with. And all of them come from homes, schools, and communities that have said, "This child is a problem, so get him out of here."

So Jimmie is staying at the training school. You might think it was an expensive private boarding school as you enter the elegant, tree-lined drive. Handsome old houses dot the well-kept grounds just as they do in novels. And you can see groups of boys engaged in ordinary school activities and can tell they're well cared for.

Inside the buildings, one group shares a reading lesson; tests show they are improving. Another group works out in the gym, and their sweat-shined bodies are in good physical condition. Another group consumes a hefty dinner in a clean dining room, and most of them return for seconds. A good school, anyone would have to conclude—well run and very orderly.

And the boys are orderly, too. They are dutiful and serious about their work, and there is no fooling around. No paper airplanes fly in this sky; no squirming wrigglers poke at one another or pass notes or visit the water fountain too often. No straws fly at the lunch table; no catsup squirts on someone's shirt. No one leaves his chair until all are excused. These boys do what they are supposed to do when they are supposed to do it.

Suddenly you know what's wrong here. These boys are too well behaved for kids eleven to fifteen years old. They get into trouble here, but when they do it is serious. They have no sense of boyish mischief. They work and play side by side, but there is no camaraderie or carefree gaiety about them. They don't smile spontaneously. But their stories, unspoken in words, can be read in their eyes, profoundly sad eyes peering out of weary little faces—the faces of old men numb to pain or joy. Their one common characteristic is their sadness.

Why are they sad? Aren't we doing what's best for Jimmie, taking him away from the social factors we know breed delinquency—his rotten home, dirty streets, lousy school, slobby friends? He needs special treatment by professionals, doesn't he? And we have put him in a wholesome atmosphere and given him all the help he needs at the training school.

This reasoning is the classic argument of a training school worker justifying his job. In these schools, we store problems on a shelf for a while. Instead of dealing with Jimmie's problems, we have got rid of them by getting rid of Jimmie. And don't think he doesn't know it somewhere deep inside himself. He may say when asked, "I'm here cause I did sumpin' bad." But his eyes tell you what he dares not admit to himself: "I'm here because nobody loves me, nobody cares, nobody wants me with all that I am, which includes my problems." You'd be sad too, if you were in his shoes.

What are Jimmie's immediate needs? Obviously, he needs remedial education. To bring him along quickly, this should be done on a tutoring basis or in a very small group where he can get continual attention and encouragement. Also, learning has to be made exciting and appealing to him. It can't be like the drudgery and regimentation of his former school, because if it is, Jimmie won't learn. He might be forced to remain physically present in the training-school classroom, but nobody can make him learn.

In addition to classroom learning, Jimmie needs good athletic training, to work off some of his youthful energy and to develop his body and coordination. He needs to have a feeling of success, which may come easier for him on the athletic field than in the classroom. Also, he needs to find pastimes—in athletics, hobbies, crafts, or school—that will be interesting and enjoyable enough so he will pursue them when he leaves, instead of waiting for trouble in the local square.

And, of course, above all Jimmie needs friends, not only young people his own age, but adult or young adult friends who can give him affection, encouragement, companionship, guidance, and caring. Without kind, responsible, adult models he can trust and respect, his chances of growing into a responsible adult are small.

There is no reason why all Jimmie's needs cannot be provided for him in his own community; that is, no reason except that we don't make the effort. It's easier for us to say, "he's somebody else's problem now."

The Training School

The chances are small that Jimmie will get what he needs in a large institution like the training school. It's likely that when he was admitted, he was given a file number, a set of sterile institutional clothes, a medical examination, and psychological tests. He was assigned to a cottage for younger boys where he got a nice clean bed and was taught how to make it properly. Then he was assigned to a classroom, where his progress or lack of it will be dutifully recorded. He got the same treatment at the gym. He was told all the things he could or couldn't do, and what he is allowed to do mainly consists of being respectful and doing exactly what he is told. In short, Jimmie was processed.

Most of the school employees will probably always be too busy processing the boys to give Jimmie individual attention. In fact, if he doesn't cause trouble, they may hardly know him. While they are corralling hundreds of boys, school workers don't have time, or the resources, to make a significant emotional investment in Jimmie. "Look, there are a hundred other kids like him. They all have problems." The employees' emotional energies have to be spread among too many people and, anyway, if they gave Jimmie the personal attention he needs, it would be regarded as favoritism. "You have to treat them all alike" in this egalitarian system. To permit Jimmie to exercise and develop his individuality would foul up the routine.

If he stays out of trouble, Jimmie will probably be paroled in about six months and will return to his own home and neighborhood. It is likely that he will go home with the same problems he had when he was sent away, except that they will be somewhat worse. Jimmie is in the training school and will return home with the undisputed reputation of a delinquent from whom good children will keep their distance. The training school won't be much help to Jimmie, or to the rest of society. He's a big boy and in a few more years will be a man. He may straighten out on his own, or he may graduate from juvenile delinquent to full-grown criminal.

Not all juvenile prisons are for boys, like Jimmie's. There are also separate institutions for delinquent girls, and institutions that have a section for boys and another for girls. I usually use the term *he* to refer to these children because, as on the adult level, most juveniles in prison are boys. Without delving into causes, which aren't clearly proven anyway, we can say that boys either engage in more mischief and crime than girls, or that they are caught more often. The treatment girls receive in state "schools," at any rate, isn't significantly different from what boys get.

It would also be inaccurate to say that the size of Jimmie's school, which houses about two hundred boys, is typical of what is found in every corner of the country. The size of institutions varies from state to state, and approximately half the states are making efforts to treat children in their own communities and to use the large training and/or industrial schools less. Some time ago, California led the way in this advance by placing a legal limit of one hundred on the number of children who could be housed in any institution, and many states have followed this example. Also, some states have closed old institutions, but still keep at least one training or industrial school open. At this time only Massachusetts has closed all its training schools, thus forcing rapid development of new resources for children in the community. Most states have one or more juvenile institutions that house more than one hundred delinquent children, and it is not unusual to find institutions with three hundred to five hundred youngsters.

This emphasis on the size of institution populations is important because, in any prison, the number of people to be supervised is closely tied to the quality of care they receive. It is especially important in centers that serve children and youth since they are still in their formative years. A small number of children in an institution is no guarantee of a high level of care and treatment. However, the reverse—a large population—almost always equals custody and warehousing, which in many ways are worse than no treatment at all for delinquent youth.

All correctional institutions, large or small, present certain built-in dangers for a child. The first, obviously, is that they remove him from everything he's familiar with. And, no matter how good the institution is, no matter how well run or how positive its philosophy, the child sees his removal from home and neighborhood as a threat and punishment. These feelings can create a threatened and insecure child whose future development is damaged.

The second danger for a child is the length of time he spends away from home. Most children remain in institutions for relatively short periods of six to eight months—a long time to a child. And, since indeterminate sentences are usually permitted by law, they can be held for longer terms if they "fail to adjust." Unfortunately, adjustment can frequently mean obedience to institutional rules and may have little or no relation to how well the child can function in the outside world.

To take a famous example, in 1964 fifteen-year-old Gerald Gault was accused of making an obscene telephone call. After a hearing in which all due process rights were ignored, he was committed to the state industrial school for the period of his minority (i.e., until 21).[1] This could have meant a six-year sentence had his parents not gone all the way to the Supreme Court. Although the Gault decision, handed down in 1967, guaranteed certain procedural rights for juveniles, children continue to go to prison for very minor offenses and for crimes such as truancy or obscenity. Frequently neither they nor their families have the knowledge, influence, or money to challenge such decisions.

Once they are in prison, some boys and girls are fortunate enough to meet with kindness, understanding, and an effort to help them with their problems and to get them home again as quickly as possible. Other children consider themselves fortunate if they are merely processed like Jimmie. And some are unlucky and find themselves in prisons administered by people whose attitudes are flagrantly punitive and whose disciplinary systems (described in nice language in the public relations brochures) would rival a marine boot camp.

In 1969, Howard James, an outstanding reporter for the *Christian Science Monitor*, researched, documented, and exposed brutal and scandalous treatment of children in state schools in three different states.[2] If he had investigated every state, he would certainly have uncovered a great deal more horror. In the same year a scandal of major proportions broke in Massachusetts juvenile institutions and led to major reform and the eventual closing of the large institutions. I haven't the slightest doubt that brutal, punitive conditions still exist in some juvenile institutions—most likely in places where citizen involvement (volunteers) is kept to a token amount, is prohibited, or is nonexistent.

Even in areas where the trend is away from large training schools, volunteers should not be lulled into thinking that the abusive conditions of old institutions are permanently eliminated. Little institutions with nice new-sounding names can also be abusive when there is no outside control. Further, since it is much easier to stash away troublesome youths than to supervise them in the community, there will always be a tendency to let those little institutions mushroom again. Once a small institution becomes crowded, one soon begins to hear, "What we need is a new and larger building." This cry should be resisted.

There is an old theory in the prison business that the number of offenders committed by the courts is suspiciously related to the number of beds that happen to be available. When all the beds are filled and the place is overcrowded, the parole board gets busy and starts releasing people who just a few weeks earlier would have been considered insufficiently adjusted. This same situation occurs in juvenile institutions. Although the theory doesn't always work perfectly, the correlation between available beds and court commitments is usually high. If beds aren't available, the courts and the community are forced to find alternate and better means of treating children. If too many beds are available, it's always easier to fill them than to engage in the more meaningful but difficult task of treating children in their own communities.

Why not get rid of all the beds? This is a good question that many people have already explored. Some have decided that at the very least there should be no large institutions for children, such as training or industrial schools. But nobody has been able to eliminate institutions entirely. Massachusetts people proudly announce they have closed all their juvenile institutions, but this isn't quite true. They have closed the ancient large training schools, and in their stead a number of group homes have been developed. Massachusetts also has a camp and three relatively secure detention centers for those juveniles "who cannot be placed" in the community.

So this is the dilemma: there are a number of youths nobody will take in a foster home, or even a group home or camp. They may have committed serious crimes, like murder, rape, armed robbery, or criminal assault. They may be sixteen or seventeen and as big, strong, mean, and scary as any adult. And they may be quite dangerous. While one can try to be understanding, I have to agree with the policeman who told me, "I feel very sympathetic about the social and emotional causes of a kid's crime, but I have to think first of protecting all the people. I'm faced with a cruel, animalistic act and with its victims. I can't say, 'It's okay, son. I know you have a tough home life.' I have to pick up the hysterical old lady who suffered a broken hip as he pushed and grabbed for her purse. Or the woman he decided to rape as well as rob." This policeman is surely going to have the offender in court very quickly. And the conscientious judge, who faces the ancient problem of balancing the rights of the community with the rights and needs of the individual, can hardly leave such a youth on the loose. The public doesn't want him wandering around either, so there has to be a place to put him.

There has been, and will continue to be, a terrible gap between the ideal of a good home for every child and the reality of those children, especially the older ones, who cannot be placed in the community. There has to be some place for delinquents to go, something for them to do. And that place is probably going to be some kind of institution—a training school, detention center, group home, or camp. If it is an ongoing organization, it is an institution. What citizens ought to be sure about is that, if institutions must exist at all, they are institutions which aren't obviously harmful and, hopefully, are helpful.

However, people tend to take the easy way out, which means there will be a tendency to make more beds available and let the juvenile warehouses flourish again. I think the only sure way to prevent this is by close, continuing citizen scrutiny and participation in the daily life of juvenile institutions. Without such participation, the public sinks into a state of apathy and fails to wake up until the next major scandal.

One way of forcing continued public involvement is to make sure only a minimum number of beds are available in any institution for children. Another way is to make certain that funds allocated by the legislature for youthful-offender care cannot be used for institutional expansion. In the case of existing institutions, it is possible to provide the minimum funds necessary without enabling the institutions to be entirely independent of the surrounding communities. This last possibility can be dangerous, however, if there is not adequate volunteer participation. The services can degenerate so much that the youths get nothing but custodial care—and the administration has a great excuse for providing nothing more. But under responsible direction, a limitation on funds can provide the impetus for extensive community involvement. Out of sheer necessity, the institution must call on community talent and bring in large numbers of volunteers.

Dependence on community involvement has been tried successfully at the Training School for Boys in Skillman, New

Jersey. If there is an institution for the young in your state—and most likely there is—the volunteer program at Skillman can serve as a model for improving it.

Skillman is a fairly new institution that opened in 1968 and was planned and headed by a man who says, "We deliberately went out to be un-self-sufficient." Since he wanted the school and community to be dependent upon one another, volunteers were sought and welcomed in every aspect of life in the school. There were no fences to keep boys in or to keep the community out. Dr. Vuocolo, the superintendent, comments, "How could you possibly rehabilitate someone for a community by locking him away from it?"

The school did not have to work very hard to get volunteers once the community knew they were needed and wanted. People usually want to help so long as somebody tells them what needs to be done, and this is exactly what Dr. Vuocolo did. More than one thousand volunteers responded, and they worked daily with the boys on the widest variety of tasks and projects found in any training school.

What, specifically, did these volunteers do? They tutored on a one-to-one basis, ran the library, and helped with arts, crafts, and hobbies. They started a botany club, a cooking club, and a rabbit club when they discovered an interest in these areas. They brought in young people from churches, schools, and youth groups to participate in sports events, arranged parties on special holidays, and gave an individual birthday party for every boy in the school. They bought athletic equipment and playground equipment and arranged for dramatic and musical performances at the school. They took groups of boys out of the school for a variety of cultural events and arranged transportation for boys who needed it to visit their homes. And in the midst of all these activities, the volunteers came to know individual boys and care deeply about them. Soon they were taking boys to their own homes, first for a day visit and then for weekends. And they maintained a continuing interest in the boys they had befriended.

There are many advantages to this kind of ongoing dependence between a school and the community. First of all, in a school where large numbers of volunteers are present on a continuing basis, there can be no opportunity for the sadistic practices found in institutions that are closed to the public. Also, the volunteers' intense interest and concern tell the boys by actions rather than words that the community has not shunned or forgotten them. It tells them that they are in the school not because everyone thinks they are bad and incorrigible, but because of a temporary problem which, with a lot of help from friends, can and will be overcome. The variety of volunteers exposes the boys to a wide range of personalities, lifestyles, and interests, knowledge of which they can take home with them. Even a good institution like Skillman is no substitute for a good home, but it certainly is a step in a good direction and an improvement over institutions that cut children off entirely from the community.

Nevertheless, I continue to be uneasy about even good juvenile institutions like Skillman. No director remains in one place forever, and what would happen to Skillman if it some day had a director who didn't want volunteers? Not every institution has a director who encourages community participation, and it is quite possible that the volunteer who wants to work in a juvenile institution will be rebuffed by the same kind of resistance common in adult institutions. The paths around the resistance are the same for both, as far as I can see, but the need to overcome it is even greater on the juvenile level than on the adult level. Not all children in prison are well treated, and while maltreatment of any human being is evil, it is particularly sadistic when suffered by children who have no chance of protecting themselves.

Camps, Ranches, and Group Homes

In most states, there are institutional alternatives to training or industrial schools: forestry camps, regular camps, ranches, and group homes. Some of these are different in nature from training schools, and others are just different in size. They are not new types of institutions, but they are increasing in number and usage in many parts of the country.

Juvenile camps or ranches vary considerably in size, housing from ten or twelve children to sixty or eighty. They are, as one can imagine, set off in the countryside, and life there is geared very much to the outdoors. Some were originally created on the theory that fresh air and exercise are good and healthy for children and should somehow make them better. Besides, how much trouble can a chap get into when there's nothing around but a forest or farm? But while the great outdoors is nice, it is not always a comfortable setting for urchins who were raised on city streets and can't feel comfortable without cement under their feet and a hangout down the block—and who always thought that milk, orange juice and green beans came from cartons. Also, large camps that are far removed from public scrutiny can degenerate into the training-school atmosphere under a new name.

Other camps, in areas where forestry or farming is the major industry and many hands are needed, were designed to put older juveniles to work. They were created on the theory that if children can't make it in school by the time they are fifteen or sixteen, they might as well learn a useful trade. The idea that needs to be examined in this case is: Is the trade useful to them or are they being used by the trade?

Some camps are experimenting with the now famous outward-bound programs. These programs are designed to improve self-confidence by proving to children that they can accomplish feats they would have thought were impossible. They are designed to foster teamwork by showing each member that he must assist others and that together the team can do what one person might never do alone. Young bullies, scared and scrawny, face something tougher than any villain on a city block. They climb mountains, endure harsh weather conditions, and ride rapids—all at the pace of the least competent member of the group. They get a real feeling of success, which is always sweet. The hope of these programs is that the self-confidence and pleasure of success the children acquire in conquering the physical world can be transferred to the seemingly hopeless social and psychological problems they will encounter back home on city streets. Outward-bound programs have been successful with nondelinquent groups and may also turn out to be quite successful with delinquents.

Group homes, the most rapidly growing alternative to training schools, are designed to be an extension of the family. They usually house a small number of children, perhaps eight or ten, and offer intensive professional counseling and support, in addition to a homelike atmosphere. Group homes are most often found in cities or suburbs not far from the child's own home and familiar surroundings. They may simply be large houses like the others in the neighborhood. They are likely to be run by a young couple, who may have children of their own in the house and who have special training enabling them to cope with delinquent youths.

But the couple is not alone. They are usually assisted by a host of specialists—probation officers, psychologists, social workers—and just plain friends (volunteers) who are trying to bring about changes in the children without removing them from their community. These workers try to provide two essentials the youths have probably lacked: some semblance of family life and individual sustained attention. The valuable characteristic of group homes is the very thing the neighbors object to: the rascals are still here and they are likely to be attending our own neighborhood school! It seems that everyone approves the idea of group homes until the agency in charge of youthful offenders decides to open one in his neighborhood.

Prison for Children

There may be no typical institution, but Jimmie is typical. No matter where you live, your state has at least one, and probably more than one, prison for children, whether it is called a school or camp or labeled with some newly invented pseudonym.

Prison for children—these are hard words to swallow, especially when we know that some children in prison are under ten years old. Perhaps you're a good parent. You love your children and can't quite believe the occasional scandalous stories you hear about kindergarten tykes sleeping in the bushes because the door is locked and Mom is out on the streets; Dickensian street urchins stealing food because they are hungry; brain-damaged infants beaten by their parents; imprisoned youngsters flogged naked and left in solitary confinement until they can "adjust." Bleeding heart stuff? Preposterous? You bet it is. The preposterous part of these stories is that they happen in every state, and these children go through juvenile court every day. Little black sheep are herded to prison with alarming regularity, the fledgling felons of the future.

No matter where we send children—to big training schools, medium-sized camps, or small group homes—we must never forget that all these facilities are to some extent seen as punitive by the children involved. Most youthful offenders are neglected rather than bad. No matter if the courts, social agencies, and society in general think a child would be better off in a nice, well-run school than in a miserable home with a delinquent parent, the child doesn't agree. Be it ever so humble, or even so cruel and damaging, home is where children want to be.

Indeed, this is the one great advantage of working with youthful offenders: no matter how antisocial their behavior may have been, they don't really want to be cut off from the mainstream of society. They are not quite so cynical as delinquent adults, and there is more hope of reformation with them, more flexibility. They want to stay with us, and they will if they can find a way to develop a stake in the community. The completely rejected child has no stake in society. Why should he? What did it ever do for him, and how much does it care about him?

To develop a stake in our society, children have to know that they are wanted, are needed, and that what they do and what they become is important. To know this, they must remain a vital part of the community, and each community must develop its own resources for them. Let's look now at what the community can do so much more effectively outside the institution, right in its own bailiwick.

PART II

OUTSIDE THE WALLS

Crime and punishment have always been associated in our thoughts with prison, the most extreme punishment short of death in our society. Attention must be paid to prisons because of the cruel consequences of incarceration and because they are remote and it is difficult to gain access to them. But it is unwise for anyone interested in criminal justice to look only at prisons. One must also examine the justice dispensed by our courts, the methods used by our police, and the inequities in the law itself. One must look to see whether or not the community has fulfilled its responsibility in eliminating the conditions that foster crime and delinquency.

Happily, most convicted offenders are not in prison. Nearly two-thirds are in the community under supervision, on probation or parole, so that the volunteer who wants to work with offenders need never set foot in a prison. If you are one of the volunteers who cannot work in a prison, you may want to read the following chapters to find a role outside the walls.

There are presently thousands of volunteers assisting the criminal justice system by their work in the courts. Most of them are working directly with young offenders who have been convicted and given probation rather than a prison sentence. Court volunteers are the largest single group of volunteers in the criminal justice system and also have the two best organizations in the system, making it relatively easy for a potential volunteer to gain entry.

7

VOLUNTEERS IN COURTS

The strong movement of volunteers in the courts began in 1959 when Keith J. Leenhouts won an election as Municipal Court Judge in Royal Oak, Michigan. He campaigned on the promise of getting a probation system started in the Royal Oak Court and lost no time after the election in fulfilling his promise. Having no money in the budget to pay a probation staff, he gathered a small group of professional friends and asked them to assist on a voluntary basis. Not only did they work voluntarily with young offenders, but they spread the word to others of the need for more volunteers, and they gradually grew into a strong and vital organization.

A similar movement started in Boulder, Colorado, in 1961 under the direction of Judge Horace Holmes, who, at that time, was unaware of what Leenhouts had done in Michigan. Both courts, finding their use of volunteers on a one-to-one basis to be quite successful, developed organizations through which the idea could spread to other parts of the country.

Today, volunteers are working in similar capacities in over two thousand courts across the country.

The small group that met in Royal Oak in 1959 grew into a national organization called Volunteers in Probation, which is now affiliated with the National Council on Crime and Delinquency. The Boulder group became the National Information Center on Volunteers in Courts. Both organizations give continuing assistance to individual courts and communities in starting and developing voluntary programs.

Though court volunteers are the largest single group of volunteers in the correctional system, not every court has volunteers or is even looking for them. There are many courts that could and should take advantage of available volunteer assistance, and I will try to show you why. But before you decide whether or not the court system is the ideal place for you to work, you will need to examine your local system to find out if you can be of assistance, and if so, how. You will need to know where the greatest needs are.

Which Court for You?

The court system in the United States is complicated, and there are variations in operations from state to state. However, in all areas, there are various levels of courts that handle different types of criminal matters.

Most criminal prosecutions occur in what are generally called the lower courts. These courts are labeled with various names and have slightly different powers depending on the state. They may be called police courts, magistrate courts, municipal or district courts, or misdemeanant courts. Sometimes they are referred to as the people's courts. They may serve only one city or one county, and some have jurisdiction in a district composed of several towns. Some of these courts, such as those in a big city, are large and busy, but many are very small. In one state, the judges may be appointed for life, and in another they may be elected for a short term.

The quality of justice dispensed in lower courts is grossly

uneven from state to state, and even from county to county. This fact is particularly distressing because the lower courts process the majority of our offenders. They are also the courts to which those who have committed minor offenses come and, in many areas, where juveniles first appear. The lower courts are the ones most likely to permit miscarriages of justice, perhaps partly because they have widely differing standards of administrative and professional competence among their personnel, including judges, and partly because the lower courts generally have no jury trial procedure for misdemeanants and no court stenographer to keep a record of what occurs during hearings or sentencing.

Lower courts suffer from a lack of money, since they are usually funded by the county, or another limited political district, rather than by the state. Thus, in most cases they have less money than the higher felony, superior, appellate, or state supreme courts. They are likely to have an inadequate probation staff or no probation service at all. It seems to me the height of irony that those accused of the most minor offenses, who come through these courts, should receive the least help and the poorest quality of justice. But a good characteristic of the lower courts is that most of them are small enough and accessible enough to be susceptible to citizen pressure.

The first requirement for a prospective volunteer is to acquire a little information about the local court, and this is not difficult to do. The quality of its administration, the quality of justice, and the quality of the services (probation) it offers the offender can be roughly assessed by talking with the local police department, the sheriff's office, local lawyers, the local newspaper editor, or the town or county officials who have continuing contact with the court. If you don't know what the standards of the court ought to be, you can compare what you find locally with the recommendations of the President's Crime Commission Report.[1] Another good source of information is your state League of Women Voters—most state Leagues have done lengthy studies on the courts. Another excellent source of information is the National Information Center on Volunteers in Courts, in Boulder, Colorado. The center has comprehensive files on those courts which already have volunteer programs, and its personnel know very well how a court should be functioning. Usually, the quality of justice in lower courts is as good or as poor as the interest the community takes in the court.

You may be fortunate enough to find a good court which already has a volunteer program in your own community. Certainly the chances of finding an ongoing program in the courts are much greater than the chances of finding them in the prisons.

As we pointed out in the earlier chapters on prison volunteers, a well-run volunteer program offers a variety of activities because offenders have varied needs and because the capabilities of volunteers are diverse. A well-run court program should do the same; it should act as an administrative funnel through which individual volunteer talents can be connected with individual offender needs. Like a good prison program, the court program should provide each volunteer with an understanding of the system in which he must function, knowledge of the offenders with whom he will work, and an appropriate amount of training and orientation for the job he is expected to do.

Probably the most popular court-connected volunteer jobs are the one-to-one relationships between volunteer and offender. Sometimes volunteers in these jobs are called sponsors, and sometimes they are known as probation aides. In some courts they are assigned only to juvenile offenders, but in others, young-adult misdemeanants are also included. In all cases, the volunteer is either assisting a probation officer who has responsibility for a large number of cases or he is filling a gap in a court that has no probation staff.

It is estimated by correctional personnel that about 10 percent of the people who come to court, some of whom go on to a prison, are seriously emotionally disturbed and need intensive professional attention. Another 15 percent need limited professional care. And 75 percent of first offenders and misdemeanants need guidance, direction, and help, but not necessarily the attention of a psychiatrist, social worker, or other highly trained professional.[2]

Some youthful offenders need an adult who is a decent

human being and can be a model for them to grow by. Others need a good listener to whom they can talk out the pain, loneliness, or alienation in their souls. And some have more specific needs, such as educational or vocational assistance. Some of the younger offenders need to be involved in recreation programs, and others need help with a drug problem, or need a temporary home. Most of them need a kind, warm adult friend to help them over the rough spots they are in. The volunteer who works in a one-to-one relationship will no doubt be assigned to one of those in the 75 percent who do not need professional assistance. What he or she does specifically with the young offender must depend entirely on his needs.

Some courts have developed their own programs for training and assigning volunteers to work with youth, and others assign volunteers only indirectly through local organizations created for the specific purpose of helping young people. Big Brother and Big Sister organizations are typical of the groups through which many courts work, and the YMCA and YWCA also play a large role in helping young offenders, as well as those who have never contemplated trouble with the law. Partners is another organization that stresses bringing adult volunteers and youth together through a program of activities the young people enjoy. The methods of administering volunteer programs and the nature of the programs depend on the needs and abilities of the court, as well as the people it serves. The important task is to involve competent volunteers in sufficient number.

So far, studies indicate that the presence of an adequate number of volunteers does make a difference in diverting young offenders from future criminal patterns. A major study was done of offenders who went through Royal Oak Court, which has a very active volunteer corps. It compared the Royal Oak group with offenders who went through another court of comparable size that had similar offenders but only one probation officer and no volunteers. A battery of psychological tests indicated that the hostility level of offenders in the Royal Oak group was significantly reduced in 73 percent of the people, compared to a reduction in only 18 percent of the offenders in the other court. The recidivism rate, which is the most commonly accepted indicator of success, was twice as high in the control court as it was in Royal Oak.[3] A similar study done in the Denver court came to the same conclusion: one-to-one relationships, which can be obtained only by employing volunteers, made a tremendous difference in averting future criminal behavior. So important is the volunteer considered by the federal government that the 1973 National Conference on Criminal Justice gave high priority to studying ways of increasing citizen involvement in all correctional programs. There is a less than gentle hint here that administrators who seek federal funds should also make volunteer programs a high priority.

One-to-one relationships require volunteers who have a lot of patience, understanding, and, in some cases, a lot of time. The term of service with a young offender may range from six months to a year, or even longer. The volunteer may see the offender twice a month or once a week, and their relationship may be relatively limited or, as often happens, they may become lifelong friends.

The volunteer who works with a probationer has no easy job. He or she is usually faced with the same kinds of social and emotional problems found in the prison offender. The difference is one of degree rather than kind of problem, but this difference has deep significance. It is the reason for some major advantages to working in a court rather than a prison.

Most court volunteers are assigned to work with either minor offenders (misdemeanants) or juveniles, which gives the volunteer a far better chance of success than he would have with people in prison. Success, in this case, equals the diversion of a young person from future criminal activities by helping him or her deal with present problems.

Professionals in the corrections field estimate that most people who commit serious crimes (felonies) began in a criminal pattern with small offenses. Most of them once went through a district or lower court in which there was no probation staff or probation volunteer. While a penalty may have been imposed on them, usually steps were not taken at that point to intervene and to offer assistance with the social or personal problems that caused their troubles.

Some young people, of course, are better off without any assistance. They are so shaken by the fact of being caught in a
criminal act that their appearance in court is a cure in itself. Surveys conducted by large probation departments support this
statement. In fact, some studies indicate that about 75 percent
of the young offenders who are given probation complete their
term of probation without further incident or trouble with the
law—some with assistance, some without.[4] However, as I
pointed out earlier, no one can be quite sure which 25 percent
will continue in a criminal pattern. When we examine the personal and social problems of inmates we meet in prisons, we're
sure to learn that a large number who graduated to worse crimes
could have been diverted from this pattern if they had received
meaningful assistance at the earlier, probationary stage.

Another reason the chances of success for the volunteer and
probationer are high is that offenders who are sentenced to probation rather than prison are a select group in the first place. Probation officers, who spend much of their time in court, should
give the judge a report on the offender prior to sentencing. This
is called a social investigation and is supposed to provide the
judge with sufficient information to decide whether or not the
offender can profit from assistance in the community rather than
a prison sentence. In some states, this report is required by law,
but in others it is rarely available. The report should contain information about an offender's family, residence, his ties to the
community and how long he has lived there, his work or school,
any previous convictions, and whether or not he has been on
probation or in prison before. The decision about who goes on
probation and who does not is, of course, made by the judge.
But most judges tend to give considerable weight to the probation officer's report. And, most of them are willing to give the
young or misdemeanant offender a second or even third chance
before committing him or her to a correctional institution—that
is, if there is a probation service available.

The presence of a good probation staff, whether they are
paid, volunteer, or a combination of both, can help increase the
court's effectiveness as a deterrent to crime. Experts seem to
agree that one of the best deterrents to crime is justice that is

fair, sure, and swift. Yet, justice in the lower criminal courts is often sloppy. If you have ever dreamed of the great American ideal of justice for all or have visions of a Perry Mason operating in every court, you can disabuse yourself of such fantasies very quickly by sitting in court as an observer for a few hours. Incidentally, any citizen has the right to do this because court sessions (except for juvenile hearings) are public business.

You may find a good court to work in, for there are many. On the other hand, you may find rudeness and incompetence in the personnel, no jury, no court stenographer, no one to give the judge information to assist him in making a just decision, illegal practices, prejudiced judges, and no probation service. Often the judge's choices may be limited to 1) a prison sentence, which may be too harsh a punishment for a minor crime; 2) a fine, which indicates to some offenders that they can buy their way out of trouble if they aren't too poor; or 3) dismissal or suspension of sentence, which may indicate to the offender that he can get away with no penalty at all and that the law is not to be paid much heed.

Adequate citizen involvement, even on the level of court observation and reporting, can help significantly in altering such situations. Charles Evans Hughes told us long ago to worry less about the high courts and "Look after the courts of the poor, who stand most in need of justice. The security of the Republic will be found in the treatment of the poor and the ignorant; in indifference to their misery and helplessness lies disaster." [5]

The lower court, the place where the volunteer is most needed, is also, happily, the most accessible of the courts. It is likely that the court nearest your home is closer than the nearest prison, so there is less traveling and time involved. Also, there is a little less hassle. Because of laws and tradition, ordinary citizens—outsiders—are more often accepted in courts than they are in prisons. Further, court volunteers are far less hampered by the myriad of rules and regulations which invariably surround a closed institution such as a prison. And, they can work with the resources of an entire community rather than within the limitations and artificial mode of life of an institution. Finally, the citizen who might be afraid to enter a prison (though the fear is

not justified) will feel much more comfortable in the less foreboding atmosphere of a court. It's not a bad place to work.

Americans have a long history of assisting one another on a
voluntary basis. It is one of the better chapters, rarely related, in
the story of the American character. Volunteers in probation
have a particular place in the world's social history, as well as in
America's, and a brief look at that history makes it easy to see
the vital importance of continuing the tradition. The entire system of probation, as we know it today, was started by a volunteer.

John Augustus and the Volunteer in Court

Few volunteers have done more for individual offenders and yet
are so little known as John Augustus. In 1841, when he began
his work with offenders, Augustus was a successful cobbler who
owned a shop near the courthouse in Boston. He was also, like
many Bostonians of that era, a dedicated member of the temperance movement. Unlike most of them, however, he was disin-
clined to sit at meetings talking about the problem. He decided
to do something, and did.

He went to the court one morning, and while observing the
parade of common drunkards being sentenced to prison, he
chose one who, though wretched in appearance, seemed to have
some hope of reformation. Augustus requested and was granted
permission to bail the man and keep him in his own care for a
period of three weeks. At the end of that time, the man was required to return to the court for possible sentencing.

Though he didn't give us many further details of the case,
John Augustus must have really put pressure on the chap. He
got him to "sign the pledge," which was quite the thing to do in
those days, apparently got him a job, and definitely cleaned him
up in both body and spirit. At the end of three weeks, "his
whole appearance was changed and no one, not even the scrutin-
izing officers, could have believed that he was the same person
who less than a month before had stood trembling on the prisoner's stand. The Judge expressed himself much pleased with

the account we gave of the man, and instead of the usual penalty,—imprisonment in the House of Correction—he fined him one *cent* and costs, amounting in all to $3.76. . . ." [6]

This was in August of 1841, and by the end of that year John Augustus had repeated this process with drunkards seventeen times with, so far as he could tell some years later, a very high rate of success at transforming them into sober and useful men. Not only was this the beginning of a new career for John Augustus, but it was the birth of the modern system of probation.

The word spread among the poor of the city that John Augustus was a man who offered real help rather than a sermon, and it wasn't long before he was swamped with requests for assistance. Though his work began because of his interest in temperance, his kindly nature soon demanded that he give assistance to persons accused of other offenses. And before his first year at court was completed, he had begun to bail out a few women, either drunkards or prostitutes. Soon he was retrieving children, quite young children, who at that time were thrown into jail with adults for minor infractions of the law. The burdens of his voluntary and solitary efforts increased so rapidly that Augustus finally turned his cobbler shop over to his son and devoted all his time to being the world's first probation officer.

Prior to his death about eighteen years later, Augustus had "bailed on probation" nearly two thousand persons and assisted thousands of others who didn't go through court but simply presented themselves at his door. He had enlisted the assistance of other citizens who gave financial support to his efforts. One group founded a home for homeless children, another a home for homeless young women, and others offered temporary shelter and/or jobs for the many people Augustus salvaged from the court.

In addition, he developed the system which is still the basis for probation officers. First, he investigated the background of the offender to determine whether the person could be helped in the community. Second, he made calls on those he had placed in the community. In one year, he made fifteen hundred calls, and over a period of time wore out a horse and three chaises. Third, he kept careful records of each person he bailed and made a report to the court on each individual's progress.

Augustus also did a little philosophizing—which eventually had a profound influence on the attitudes of the court toward offenders. It was he who proposed that the "object of the law is to reform criminals and prevent crime and not to punish maliciously or from a spirit of revenge." [7] Of course, many people still don't agree with this purpose of the law, but this philosophy became, and continues to be, the foundation of the modern system of probation.

As a direct result of the successful work of John Augustus and several other volunteers who continued the work after his death, Massachusetts passed the first probation law in 1878, which outlined the duties of a paid probation officer. The idea spread gradually throughout the country and the world, but probation systems didn't become law in every state until about one hundred years after Augustus first entered the court.

Curiously enough, the role of volunteers declined as probation became the law of the land. When probation officers were recognized with salaries, and it appeared they were doing the job, volunteers turned their attentions to other areas of social need. This is unfortunate because, as the system became accepted and entrenched, it also became a bureaucracy. People presumed that because a law had been passed and another salary had been placed on the tax rolls, the work was being done effectively. For a number of reasons, this presumption was erroneous.

First, the probation officers were generally appointed by the presiding justice. In many cases, the appointments were good ones, but there were—and still are—many cases in which such appointments degenerated into patronage plums for friends who wanted a secure job. Such persons showed little interest in helping offenders.

Secondly, many of the district courts didn't have enough money—and still don't—to employ enough probation officers to do the job of supervising offenders properly. In many jurisdictions there were—and still are—no probation officers at all. In others, it was—and continues to be—common for one probation officer to have from one hundred to three hundred offenders in his charge. Obviously, the officer couldn't even keep track of so many people, never mind supervise or give them the assistance many of them need. Many probation officers do paper work and record-keeping, and have very little direct contact with the people they are supposed to help.

Another reason the number of volunteers declined sharply is that they were pushed out in subtle ways. As the probation system grew, the volunteer citizen came to be seen as something of a threat to the paid personnel. Also, as the system became slightly professionalized, the citizen was denigrated on the assumption that this was work for highly trained professionals and that volunteers were not qualified to deal with difficult social problems.

This latter reaction was old-fashioned bull throwing, because the fact is that only in the last couple of decades have specific requirements of education and experience become standard for probation officers. The standard is yet to be universally applied, and while it is essential to improve and professionalize probation service, it shouldn't cause professional snobbery. The ability to relate to other human beings has yet to be preempted by the educated. Professionalization need not and should not obviate the need for additional assistance and support from volunteer citizens.

In spite of the fact that court volunteers are numerous and fairly well organized, there are still pockets of resistance to volunteer participation. The potential volunteer shouldn't expect every court to welcome him or her with open arms, as the naïve might expect. Just as the prison volunteer must be prepared to encounter some staff hostility, so must the volunteer in court. There are many people in courts who are more concerned with job security than with helping the offender, and, to such persons, the volunteer continues to look like a threat. If you think this is not so, permit me to offer you an excerpt from a letter from Mary Pickman, Director of the volunteer Legal Advocate Program of New York City. The letter was printed in the newsletter of the Volunteers in Probation and had a 1972 dateline.

The purpose of the Board of Correction's Legal Advocate Program is to address the problems of the City's Criminal Justice System as they affect the prisons. One of the most severe problems is the delay between conviction and sentence caused by the inability of overburdened probation departments to prepare the pre-sentence reports which are required by statute to be submitted to the judge before sentence is passed. The problem is most severe in Kings County (Brooklyn). There are currently 850 defendants who have been convicted in Kings County Supreme Court for crimes for which they should be sentenced to upstate institutions, but who remain in the City's detention facilities awaiting sentence.

In order to address this problem, we wrote to the administrative judge in Kings County offering to recruit a group of volunteer lawyers and law students to work on a part-time basis in the Kings County Department of Probation assisting in the conduct of pre-sentence investigations and preparing pre-sentence reports. We were invited to proceed and organized a group of 15 volunteers, half practicing lawyers and half law students, who began work in the Department of Probation on August 14, 1972. Each volunteer was assigned three or four cases and given the responsibility for gathering information on the defendant's present offense, any mitigating or aggravating circumstances, the defendant's previous criminal history, and his background. The volunteers also were given the responsibility of interviewing each defendant and for preparing a draft of the pre-sentence report, to be submitted to a supervising probation officer for review and criticism.

On the same day that the volunteers began working, *the Probation and Parole Officer's Association of Greater New York, Local 599, filed suit against us to restrain the volunteer effort. The Union's petition alleged that the use of volunteers violated the New York State Civil Service Laws and constituted an unfair labor practice. We understand that the Union's suit was motivated by a fear that the use of volunteers would preclude the hiring of more probation officers. The case turned upon a factual issue, namely, whether our volunteers were performing all the ordinary and necessary duties of qualified probation officers. Our contention was that the effort of the volunteers was strictly min-

*isterial in that it was restricted to the gathering of data and inter-
views of defendants, and did not call for the exercise of professional discretion.*

*At a hearing held in the Kings County Supreme Court on
September 13, 1972, the judge dismissed the Union's petition. . . .*[8]

Of course, though this volunteer group went to a good deal
more trouble than is ordinarily required, their case exemplifies
the level of hostility which may be encountered. Sometimes the
hostility is hidden and never openly stated. Their story also indicates who really cared about the offenders; in this case, as in so
many, it was the volunteers and not the people who were paid
for their services.

Hostility between volunteers and court officers isn't a new
problem. In fact, John Augustus faced a similar problem back in
1842. For some time, he couldn't understand why the court
officers in the Police Court gave him such a difficult time and
on occasion even threw him out of the court bodily. Then he
made the marvelous discovery that court officers were paid 75
cents every time they delivered a prisoner to the jail. Every person John Augustus rescued was just 75 cents lost as far as they
were concerned. And remember, in those days the dollar went a
long way.

Money still talks, it often appears, but don't let that stop
you from working in a probation program or even starting one if
necessary. Sometimes a court program begins with the efforts of
a dedicated judge reaching out to citizens for help. Often, programs begin because of a dedicated group of citizens who put sufficient pressure and determination on the court and local judge.

An endless number of programs can be started by individuals, given enough persistence. But programs can produce little of
significance in a court without a genuine spirit of cooperation
among judges, the probation staff (if there is one), and the citizens who volunteer. Many experienced professionals agree that
without such cooperation, volunteer programs will either fail or
will exist as token concessions to a growing tide of citizen concern. Either of these alternatives wastes time and energy.

The judge is generally the key to success or failure of a probation program, especially where volunteers are concerned. Not only is his word law in the daily procedure of the courtroom itself, but he is usually the boss to any paid staff, including probation officers. He can and often does make his will felt, so cooperation of the judge is the most vital factor in a successful volunteer program.

Some judges still regard volunteer programs with less than enthusiasm. Some need to be nudged by a stubborn group of citizens. And, help on the nudging process, for anyone who wants it, can be obtained from the National Information Center in Boulder or from Volunteers in Probation in Royal Oak. It is a good idea to seek such help, since it is rare indeed for a modern John Augustus to start or carry out a program singlehandedly.

Bail Projects

Some people would like to assist offenders but would find it hard to sustain the ongoing relationship necessary to a probation program. If you fit into this category, there are other important areas of work to be done in the court. One of them is the type of program connected with the bail system. These are usually called bail-reform projects or release-on-recognizance programs.

The system of money bail is a very old one and was originally designed as a form of assurance that the accused person would show up for his trial. This assurance continues to be the only legal justification for requiring money bail. However, in practice, the bail system is also used as a form of preventive detention. The amount of money required for bail is most frequently determined by the seriousness of the alleged crime. The amount of bail can also depend on the attitude of the judge toward certain groups of people and certain kinds of offenses. In practice, high bail does not interfere with the most serious criminals. Members of organized crime can get the money together very quickly. Bail practices do hurt the poor defendant who cannot muster even a small amount of money. He or she must await trial in the local jail, the consequences of which are serious.

In 1961, the Vera Institute of Justice, a private organization in New York City, pioneered the kind of bail-reform project which has since spread to many parts of the country. Our system of justice would take a giant step forward if such projects existed in every court. The Vera Institute developed a short standard form which gives the judge enough information about the accused person so he can make an intelligent decision about the chances of the defendant appearing in court at the appointed time. The volunteer interviews the accused as he awaits his turn for a preliminary hearing. The volunteer may also check out by telephone the information he is given about the individual's family, residence, employer, whether the defendant is enrolled in school, and whether he or she has any previous convictions. Based on this information, judges may decide to release defendants either on their own recognizance or in the technical custody of a relative or friend. The process takes about twenty minutes, so a busy court would require quite a number of volunteers to do the job properly.

The records compiled by the Vera Institute reveal several interesting facts. First, the vast majority of those who were released before trial did appear in court as required. Those who were released on recognizance actually appeared in a higher percentage than those released on money bail. Secondly, the likelihood of the defendant appearing for trial seems to be much more closely connected to a stable position in the community than it does to the crime he committed. Thirdly, we are all influenced by appearances: those who arrived in court via the prisoner's dock after a period in jail were much more likely to be convicted than those who came freely on their own.[9] The people who did not await trial in jail had many other advantages as well. They did not lose contact with their families. They did not lose a job or have to drop out of school. And they had the time and freedom to get a good lawyer, to find witnesses, and generally to prepare a better case for their day in court. For the court itself, the most obvious advantage is that it brings our system a little closer to the professed ideal of equal justice for rich and poor alike.

Court-Resource Projects

There is yet another kind of program, which has some characteristics of the one-to-one sponsorship and some traits of the bail
projects. It may go by different names in different places—
court-resource or court-services or court-employment project.
The programs themselves vary slightly from place to place, but
their essential nature is similar, and some of them depend very
heavily on volunteers.

The idea in a program of this kind is to spot the first
offender or the minor offender and do something to divert him
from crime before he has a conviction and record to carry with
him for life. Screeners, who may be either volunteer or paid,
work in the court doing much the same work John Augustus
did: they try to spot those who are likely to profit from assistance. They get background information on those persons and
talk to them about the possibilities of counseling, education, vocational training, or employment. When the screener decides he
has a likely candidate for assistance, he requests a continuance
of the case for a certain period, usually about ninety days.

During this period, the defendant becomes part of the project, which is usually composed of a team of professionals who,
after considerable analysis of the individual's problems, create a
program for him to follow. Like everything else, the program
varies according to the needs of the individual: education, employment, or whatever. The team also gives the person guidance
and supervision during the ninety days. If, during this time, the
defendant follows the program set out for him, and is doing
well, the case against him is dropped, and he has no conviction
record to handicap him for life. It is a sort of intensive probation
plan prior to conviction, rather than after the fact, and it is
growing in favor in many courts.

It seems to many people, including me, that there is great
wisdom in fostering the growth of court-resource projects. The
purpose of the court is to resolve conflicts between individuals
and groups. Laws are written to prevent anticipated conflicts.

The whole idea of corrections is to prevent repeated conflicts with the law and with fellow citizens. If, as a society, we are ever to relinquish our ancient desires for pure revenge and truly to embrace the concept of corrections, we must think continually of prevention of crime and delinquency. Prevention works better in a court than a prison; better prior to conviction than afterwards. Indeed, prevention best begins in the community itself long before conflicts are brought to a court of law.

If prison or court programs don't or can't provide the right kind of work for you, consider for a while the much more difficult work of crime prevention.

Prevention is difficult because we have only a few guidelines to go by, most of which have not been fully tested. It is difficult because there is no single solution on which we can spend a million dollars and then consider the problem settled. It involves the very spirit of a community, which, in many cases, needs radical change. It can't be bought, and it requires a host of willing, patient, hardworking citizens to bring it about. The task can be monumental.

Most people in the criminal justice system agree that offenders must be held responsible for their transgressions, and we hold them responsible by a network of criminal laws and sanctions. Without this we could all, with impunity, wreak havoc on society. However, everyone I've met who works regularly with offenders also agrees that there are extenuating circumstances in most instances of crime, especially among those who are habitual offenders. There are many causative factors in the community which are susceptible to change. There are slums and grinding poverty, which keep large groups of people in a continuing state of desperation and hostility; there are racial tension and class prejudice; a lack of facilities to occupy the young, and bad schools; and there are bad and negligent parents. Of all these causative factors, the single most important one is the family. Thus,

8

THE TASK OF PREVENTION

the community can disclaim responsibility by saying, "Well, it's the family he comes from. What can we do about it?" This attitude is a great excuse for doing nothing, and it is based on a very narrow view of the relationships among human beings.

I am not willing to let the community off the hook so easily. I agree that the family is most important. However, I believe firmly that the quality of family life is most intimately connected with the quality of community life. Crime statistics, such as they are, appear to bear this out. Crime distribution maps show that most crime is concentrated in areas where social conditions and the quality of community life are worst.

It is true conceit on our part to imagine that we are so independent that we may take total personal credit for the brains or talent, goodness or success we have. Some of these attributes were given at birth, some acquired from our families. Habits were formed in us by others; we were influenced by an environment. How, then, can we assume that individual families are not seriously affected by the conditions that surround them? Are marriages not affected by money problems as well as love? Are children not influenced by the neighbors and the teachers in school as well as their parents? Do we not live by the standards of the community as well as the family? I recall an example from my childhood.

Many years ago, Father Flanagan, founder of Boys' Town, said, "There's no such thing as a bad boy." I was a child then, and I thought Father Flanagan was wrong. After all, there was Bobby in my class. He was a bad boy. Well, none of the big people actually said so, but the teachers always had Bobby in disgrace for something or other, and we knew he wasn't one of the kids we were supposed to bring home after school.

Bobby came to school when he felt like it, which was mostly during bad weather. On nice spring days, he said he was sick, but we knew he was off lolling in the long grass with his Saint Bernard. Bobby forged absence excuses from his mother, which the rest of us didn't dare do. He annoyed the teachers—always bringing his dog to school, letting him howl outside the window on snowy days, and saying that the only way to stop the howling was to let him in. He was smart, but only sometimes did his homework. And sometimes, when the teachers nagged and nagged at him, he sassed them back. He seemed to spend an awful lot of time sitting outside the principal's office. None of us ever met.his parents, but there were many rumors about them. It was said that one was an alcoholic and that his father was always whipping him.

I don't recall that any of us disliked Bobby. In fact, we sort of admired him from a distance and were a little in awe of him. Some of us wished we had the courage to bring our dogs to school. We envied other things, too. Bobby was allowed to wander to all sorts of places at all hours when we couldn't. He could hang around town when we had to report home. He saw every movie that came to town, and he had a fantastic supply of comic books. He said his dog was even allowed to sleep with him. And his mother let him go to the drugstore for lunch all the time so he could eat all the junk he wanted. His life seemed very exciting to us.

But we didn't play with Bobby very often because parents discouraged it—a bad influence. Except for his dog, Bobby was almost always alone. He was our modern Tom Sawyer, except that he always looked sad, and he wasn't so poor as Tom. But even as kids, we knew that Tom Sawyer's style was only for the long, lazy vacations. You couldn't grow up like that. It just wouldn't be right. We expected that Bobby would come to no good, and that he would go to reform school, wherever that was, because he didn't pay attention to anybody—even the principal, who was the fiercest woman I have ever known.

I lost track of Bobby after fifth grade, so I don't know whether he ever fulfilled our expectations by becoming a formally adjudicated delinquent, but I wouldn't be surprised. Not that Father Flanagan was wrong, mind you, or that Bobby was particularly evil. I realize now that Bobby wasn't a bad boy; he just seemed bad to us at the time because he didn't have to live by very strict standards. However, I also realize that Bobby suffered through the basic conditions which encourage delinquency. The most important influences on Bobby's life—on any child's life—the family, the school, and the community, were doing very little for him. If he grew into a fine man, it would have been in spite of them, not because of them.

There was clearly the lack of a cooperative and caring spirit, a good sense of community, to surround and help Bobby overcome the handicaps he had in his family. This lack of spirit disables us in any attempt to deal with potential problems or with already existing problems. When people are in difficulty, they are rarely given the feeling that the community around them stands ready and willing to help. Instead, the community stands ready to condemn. Therefore, our general tendency is to hide problems until they become so serious they can no longer be hidden. At that point, what was once a problem becomes a disgrace. We feel disgraced if the family alcoholic becomes known, disgraced if we have marital problems, disgraced if a child isn't doing well in school, disgraced if we are out of a job. Then we become hostile, and it's the old, sorry story of "me against the world." It doesn't help anyone.

The Importance of Family

Of course, everyone knows how important a child's family is. Even as children, we instinctively sensed the seriousness of Bobby's family problems. If what we heard about his family was true, Bobby's start in life was a very poor one. The discipline his father administered was not fair, firm, and kindly, as it should have been. It was erratic, and violent when the mood struck, and nonexistent when his father chose not to be bothered with Bobby. The supervision of his mother was almost nonexistent. In fact, that is why Bobby was given all the freedom we envied. His mother didn't much care where he was so long as he didn't bother her. There didn't seem to be much affection from his parents, and there wasn't much sign of family unity. They didn't do anything as a family. Indeed, they seemed like an unrelated trio hanging their hats in the same boardinghouse. I've sometimes thought that Bobby's wonderful dog, his constant companion, may have been his salvation. The dog was the only being that

Bobby really seemed to care about, and that makes good sense because the poor beast seemed the only one who cared for Bobby.

The question remains as to what can be done about problem families like Bobby's. One can't just march in, tell them they are no good, and take over the reins. Official intervention by social agencies is dangerous. When children are singled out for special treatment by official agencies (because it is predicted they will, or might, become delinquent), they are labeled problem children. Sometimes they are derided and avoided by other children. The labeled child then reacts, usually with hostility. A chain of action and reaction occurs in which the child becomes what people said he would become—he lives up to what is expected of him and fulfills the predictions. Official intervention by social agencies often makes matters worse.

In Bobby's case, and in many cases, there could easily have been some unofficial intervention by the community. Certainly his family problems were well known. My parents could have encouraged him to spend more time with our family. We could have drawn him into a family fold instead of keeping him out. Instead of perceiving this as special treatment, Bobby would simply have understood that others liked him and cared about him, and he would have loved it. But the helping spirit wasn't there. It did not exist in the school either. Teachers, who knew his problems, could have helped with kindness and understanding—even some tolerance of his old mutt—but they did not.

Unlike Bobby, some children do need help from official sources. The most drastic form of intervention, of course, is the removal of a child from his parents' home. Generally, this occurs in rather extreme situations in which the child is being grossly physically abused. Battered children, or babies so neglected they are starving to death, are brought into large city hospitals with terrifying regularity. Failure to remove them from extremely delinquent parents would probably result either in their death or permanent physical damage.

However, removing a child from his natural parents is an extreme act, is always dangerous to the child's development, and should be chosen only when it is clearly the lesser of two evils. There are many borderline cases, cases similar to Bobby's, in which this extreme action is taken. Such action could frequently be avoided if communities were more generous in spirit.

Recently, the police were called to "do something" about two preschool children who were running about the neighborhood naked on a chilly day. When the policeman knocked at the door of their home at 11:00 A.M., the mother was difficult to rouse. She was sleeping off the alcohol from the previous night's spree. The policeman did the only thing he could: brought the children inside, made certain the mother would remain awake and vertical, asked her to dress them, and left the scene.

In a private conversation some days later, the policeman, who is a kindly soul, said that the woman drinks a great deal and the children are often neglected. He felt that the children should be taken away from her, and complained that the legal process for removing them was long and difficult and probably wouldn't be successful, since no actual crime could be proven.

This story raises two issues. First, the legal process of removing children from their homes should be long and difficult. Imagine the consequences if it were ever made easy. Officialdom of many varieties would soon be poking into our private lives telling us how we ought to be living, working, thinking, and bringing up our children. We would soon be functioning like robots, according to some bureaucrat's idea of what is proper. Arbitrary intervention in private life has always been vigorously fought in America, and we hope that it always will be.

The second issue is: Where was the supportive community that would lend a helping hand to this woman? What sort of neighbor would call the police over such a matter? Why couldn't the neighbor have taken the children by the hand, as the policeman did, dressed them, made a cup of coffee for the woman, and maybe talked to her and tried to help? Why? Is there hatred? Is there such fear of a sleeping woman and two little children? Is it, well, not my business? Is it fun to have a bit of scandal at someone else's expense? Is it exciting to see the police car come?

What does your community do, what informal, nonofficial

ways do you have for helping problem families? Well-adjusted children are the products (usually) of happy husbands and wives and families. Alcoholic parents are usually miserably unhappy people trying to bury their problems in a bottle. If I were a troubled spouse or parent in your community, what help could I get? Would I have to go to some official agency, which the people most in need of help won't do? How could I get competent help without feeling embarrassed or disgraced? Do your local churches or an ecumenical council of churches have regular, ongoing discussion groups or rap sessions on marital and family problems? Does your high school offer preparation for marriage for young people? Do existing informal groups make an effort to reach out to those who are not group joiners? Is there a spirit of cooperation and helpfulness in the neighborhood, or is it each man for himself? Would you, individually, as a neighbor, have reached out to help the woman and her children, or would you, too, have called the police? Is yours a community, like so many, in which couples suffer in quiet desperation and ultimately take it out on their children by abuse or neglect?

The Influence of School

The school is second only to the family as a major influence in a child's development, and it is the most significant institution through which one can informally judge the quality of community spirit. Since the school is the only place in the community through which all children pass, it is the one place where we can observe the quality of life parents demand for their children. It is also the only place in the community with which most adults have contact. Therefore, given leadership and cooperation, it is the most favorable spot to develop a genuine sense of sharing and concern among citizens for each other and for their children. It ought to be the hub around which a multitude of activities revolve. It is an excellent vehicle through which troubled people—adults and children—and people who are on the fringe of trouble can be reached. It does not represent official intervention in the private lives of citizens, it is not coercive, and it is not condemnatory. Better use of the school offers no disadvantages and many potential advantages.

I cannot help but think that most of our school systems could do a better job than they presently do in diverting young people from criminal acts and helping children deal with family problems. As I say this, I can feel the eyebrows rise and the verbal brickbats begin to fly. As one teacher put it, "Look, that's not my responsibility and I'm not trained in criminology or psychiatry. I'm here to teach."

True enough. But to teach children, of course. And children who have severe problems in their families are often difficult to teach. Their minds are elsewhere. They may receive no encouragement at home, and they may be nervous and fearful. They may be hostile. So what good is teaching if a youngster has too many problems which prevent learning? It's no good. And for what purpose are we teaching children? Is it just to recite lessons, or is it to help them to grow into decent adults who are also educated, thinking human beings?

In fact, we know that a very high percentage of those who become delinquent are school dropouts, young people who were made miserable in school. They were not helped. Schools and teachers cannot evade responsibility for offering personal help to children, for it is part of education just as academic achievement is—perhaps a greater part. A long-perpetuated myth which cannot die too soon is the idea that special professional training in psychiatry or criminology is required to spot or assist a child with troubles. All that is required in millions of instances is a warm, perceptive human being, and many teachers claim these qualities. These characteristics are not sufficient to deal with seriously disturbed children, but they are enough for most kids. I'm sure they would have worked wonders with Bobby.

Many children who grow into delinquency are so much like Bobby it frightens me. Bobby wasn't stupid; he was quite clever. But his family problems followed him everywhere, and showed themselves in school in his hostility to teachers. Instead of helping him, the teachers perceived him as a threat to their precious authority and kept sending him to vegetate outside the principal's door. No wonder boys like Bobby so often drop out of school. It isn't the kind of treatment anyone enjoys.

And what can the school do for the Bobbys of this world? Any teacher can tell you that the problem parents—the ones a teacher might wish to talk with—are the ones who never come to the school. They don't attend PTA or other school activities, and some of the more recalcitrant ones do not even respond to a teacher's letters or calls. Some don't care. Others rightly suspect they are being called to discuss a problem, and they don't want to face it; they are afraid, guilt-ridden, or intimidated. There will, no doubt, always be a hard core of delinquent parents who will remain unreachable by informal means. However, I am convinced there is a substantial fringe around that hard core who could be helped in dealing with parent-child problems if there were a more favorable atmosphere of cooperation between schools and parents.

Mrs. Smith is an example. Mrs. Smith has four young children, the oldest of whom is Paul, who is in sixth grade. Mr. Smith is drinking heavily and has received warnings from his employer that his job performance is poor and that he may be replaced if he doesn't shape up. The Smiths' marital relationship is badly strained, and they are both venting their frustrations on the children. To top it off, Paul is bringing home report cards which are progressively worse. Mrs. Smith, deep inside, knows the situation is moving beyond her control. She needs help to cope with it, but she doesn't know where to turn. She is desperately trying to hide her husband's problem from the neighbors and has withdrawn from conversation with them. She's independent and never goes to agencies for anything. She wouldn't call the school for help because she is intimidated by those "educated people." Also, she thinks there is something disgraceful and disloyal in talking about her husband's problem. If she did, everybody would know about their problems, and Paul would be made to suffer in some way that she can't define, but feels in her bones.

As a result, the situation will continue to degenerate until there is a family crisis. Perhaps Mr. Smith will lose his job, and they will have to go on welfare. Perhaps he will land in jail for drunken driving or assault one of his family while under the influence of alcohol. The school might demand to see Mrs. Smith when Paul's performance or behavior becomes really bad. As she says, "When the principal's office calls, you know it means trouble."

It doesn't have to be this way. Suppose the school system had developed a different system of reporting to parents, as many school systems have already done. Suppose that, instead of sending home a cold, sterile, almost inhuman report card full of numbers or letters four times a year, the school required at least one personal, individual private conference with the parent. Some schools require three and four conferences per year.

What would happen? There would continue to be a hard core of delinquent, disturbed, incompetent parents who would not come to such personal conferences. However, teachers would meet and have a chance to talk with the fringe people like Mrs. Smith. It is estimated that the school would make personal contact with up to 20 percent more parents than it now sees.

So what? What does the school do with the contact, once established, that it did not do by sending home a report card? Doesn't the school's primary responsibility, academic education, remain the same? Of course. But the system of private parent-teacher conferences, if gradually and properly developed, can change the spirit of a school. It can help close the artificial dichotomy between home and school and help eliminate the attitude which says, "This much is my job, and that much is their responsibility."

A child cannot be broken into compartments in which his emotional life is at home and his intellectual life at school. The school must be seen as an extension of the home, for the job of parents and schools is the same. Both have the responsibility of raising and educating an intellectually and spiritually whole human being. Since the influence of the school on a child's growth and development is second only to that of his home, close cooperation between the two is the only way a child can get the best from both.

The difference between the private parent-teacher conference and the sterile report card is like the difference between frequent conversations with a friend and a once-a-year letter that says, "Hi. Have been awfully busy doing this, this, and this. Hope you are well. Will write again next year." Such letters do nothing to foster friendship, because friendship depends very little on the exchange of factual information. It depends far more on sharing how we feel about facts, how we react to the world around us, how we share what is in the deeper recesses of our souls. When we converse directly with a friend, we hear more than the words (the facts). We hear nuances, tones, feelings in the voice. We see expressions in the face and body which often tell us more than words. We can communicate and reveal the self more easily and quickly, more honestly and thoroughly. The private conference, though obviously not on the same level of intimacy as the conversation of two friends, has some of the same advantages.

Look at the Mrs. Smiths of the world under the conference system. All parents have been notified that the school is going to try the conference system. Specific days are set aside for the purpose, and individual appointments are made with each parent. Neither Mrs. Smith nor her son is being singled out in any way; it's just a method of building closer cooperation with all parents. Since the conferences are for everyone, she doesn't have to feel intimidated. She is still a little nervous about talking to those "educated people," but she is a parent who wants to do what she is "supposed" to do for her children. If the school says you are supposed to come for a conference, she will come.

Upon arrival for the conference, Mrs. Smith discovers that Paul's teacher is very pleasant and not difficult to talk with, as she had imagined. In fact, she has a son of her own and seems to enjoy the shenanigans of boys of this age. They discuss Paul's performance in school, and Mrs. Smith feels pleasure in hearing that teachers regard Paul as being quite bright and a pleasant boy to work with.

"I wish he was like that at home," says Mrs. Smith. "I have to keep after him and after him to make him do his chores. And he's gotten real fresh about it."

As it turns out, he's not doing all his chores in school either, since his performance is slipping. However, this is expressed to

Mrs. Smith in a positive fashion, such as, "We think Paul could be doing better work than he is doing." Mrs. Smith can accept this easily because it is presented in a positive framework. She got the good news about him first. The tone of voice and the expression say to her, "We are here to see your son do the best he can." It is not threatening to her. It is encouraging.

At this point, the teacher and Mrs. Smith can explore together the possible causes of Paul's poor performance. They can explore cooperatively the kinds of actions each can take to help the boy. Each contributes something to the other's knowledge and understanding of this child because each is viewing him under different conditions. Though nothing specific may be said about Mr. Smith, the teacher may get the sense that all is not well at home, and she may put a little less pressure on Paul at school. Mrs. Smith discovers that Paul has more potential than she had given him credit for, and she may find that positive encouragement and praise are more effective than nagging.

At the end of the conference, the central problem of Mr. Smith's drinking probably hasn't been touched, but a level of understanding and cooperation has been reached. The school and teacher will be less threatening to Mrs. Smith in the future. There is someone who seems competent and in whom she has confidence. Mrs. Smith might call the teacher and she might talk to her at a future conference. Even if she does talk with the teacher, the problem will not be resolved. But often, talking out a problem helps us see it in better perspective and cope with it a little better. Nobody expects the teacher to know how to cure a man who is diving headfirst into alcoholism. But a good listener, a perceptive human being, might be able to give Mrs. Smith the confidence, courage, and maybe the know-how or know-where to seek competent help.

In the meantime, Mrs. Smith and the teacher are at least giving one another clues about the reasons for Paul's poor performance. Very often in human behavior, just as in medicine, we can't cure, but we can alleviate the severity of symptoms. It's possible that Paul may have to learn to live with the problems caused by an alcoholic father. We cannot be sure that Paul will be successful, but we can be sure he doesn't have a chance of coming through unscathed without the support and understanding of helpful adults. What the personal conference has done is open a possibility for understanding and assistance that would not otherwise have existed. In the long run, it may contribute more to Paul's learning ability, to his capacity to benefit from the teacher's teaching, than all the reading, writing, and arithmetic she could give him.

The conference system is, administratively, more difficult than the sterile report card. It takes more time in thoughtful preparation, more time in setting up and keeping appointments. But when one ponders the possible benefits, it seems well worth the effort.

One of my favorite school principals says, "We are not here to foster our own narrow interests. We are here for the children. And only by working in very close cooperation with parents can we break down the artificial barriers between school and home. A school should be a warm and happy place to which children look forward each day. Home should be a place to which they return happily. If such an atmosphere is missing from either place, there is not a healthy environment for growing children."

Some of the factors which contribute to crime and delinquency, such as poverty, must be attacked on a national scale. It is difficult for us as individuals to do a great deal about such problems, beyond writing to our congressmen. We feel helpless and frustrated. One of the nice things about a community and a school is that they are close enough, familiar enough, and small enough to be influenced and improved. The attitudes found in your school system are a reflection of your entire community, an indicator of whether or not you have a good environment for children. How is the school in your community?

Community Activities

It is a simple statistical fact that teenagers account for a percentage of crime vastly out of proportion to their numbers in the general population. The teens are a difficult and dangerous age, when young people have achieved some degree of independence from their parents, but haven't yet matured enough to use it. Some teenage crime is surely committed by young hoodlums who are well on their way to a life of crime. But a lot of it is committed by kids who are basically good and simply have an abundance of energy, mischief, time on their hands, rebellious feelings, and a lack of sense and direction. Not all, but a large part, of this teenage crime could be prevented by providing adequate community facilities and activities to satisfy some of the special needs of teenagers.

Some of the programs I am about to suggest obviously cost money. However, the costs don't have to be prohibitive, and the amount these facilities and activities cost is well worth the expenditure. Look at your own community to see how many of these suggestions are implemented. A few communities, a very few, may have all of them available for their youth. Some communities don't need all these programs, but every community should have at least some of them.

Do you have good vocational training for those who are not academically inclined? This kind of program must be run professionally and is costly. However, it should be high on any community's priority list, since vocational training is extremely important for the large number of students who are presently made to feel like failures if they don't finish an academic course. When students feel this way they do not develop a strong stake in the community, and this is an important source of dissatisfaction and potential trouble. Such young people should be learning trades and crafts and perhaps entering small business ventures, developing skills of which the community can be proud. Outcasts we don't need; skilled tradesmen we need desperately.

Even in an official school program, costs can be held down and community spirit can be improved by the inclusion of able, talented members of the community. For example, you can increase the variety of vocational training opportunities, even when a certain vocation is not hotly pursued by a large number of students. A community can easily hire, on a part-time basis, able-bodied, knowledgeable retired persons. It can't cost a great deal because their earning capacities are limited in the first place. Many older people who feel desperately useless and have lost the joy and hope of life would even be happy to donate their talents on a volunteer basis.

I think of an elderly man I knew who was a master bookbinder, trained in Europe in the days when one had to know every minute aspect of a craft and had to serve a long apprenticeship before being permitted to work at full salary—a rare person in modern times. He was retired, physically healthy, spiritually miserable, and would have raced daily to a high school to teach his art to any youth interested. Even one good student would have made his life happy. But he didn't have a degree in education, they said. The local law required that all high school teachers have certain degrees. And, they didn't use volunteers. So the youths and the man and the community all lost that lovely talent, to the detriment of all of them. A degree, indeed! Need we be so small in vision and spirit that we can't recycle the talent under our very noses?

Another school-connected opportunity that can be made available without excessive expense is a work-study program. This activity enables students to gain both money and experience. It is an excellent program for students who are temporarily weary or discouraged with school, as well as for those who have a serious need for funds. It is also a way for local merchants and manufacturers to become more closely involved with the needs of young people, and it keeps a student who might drop out of everything in continuing contact with people in a position to help him.

Are there well-supervised and well-equipped sports facilities in your community? Obviously, some facilities, such as an olympic swimming pool, can be pretty expensive. But if the community can afford it, such a facility can be well worth the cost. If it is centrally located—in a school, for example—there is no good reason why cooperative arrangements can't be made with the town or city to make it available to all the citizens on a staggered schedule.

Not every community can afford such facilities, but all can afford to offer more than a broken-down basketball hoop. One town, which said it had no funds for a baseball diamond, had a spirited group of fathers. With permission of the town, they constructed the diamond themselves on town property. Then they organized and voluntarily coached teams of pint-sized players. Everyone could play; no one was rejected. The quality of the baseball may have left something to be desired, but the quality of spirit was extremely high.

Even in an inner city, groups of willing citizens can turn empty lots into places for street hockey, basketball, or tennis. Citizens can also do the major work of supervising play areas and keeping them open afternoons, evenings, and weekends when youngsters have a lot of free time. There is little good in having a facility if it is not accessible.

In one suburban town, I found that fine young hockey teams, which played under supervision four nights a week, were entirely coached and supervised by volunteers who simply loved hockey. There are many citizens who like sports, are good at them, and would gladly coach and supervise the young, if they were asked. To many people it would be a joy.

Is there any effort made to get teenagers and younger children to work or play alongside adults in your community? Or are teenagers, parents, and the elderly all treated as separate species? Are there activities that can attract a whole family? For example, is the school gymnasium for use only during school hours, or is it available for father-son games on evenings and weekends? Could the gym be used for an occasional rock-and-roll dance, a square dance, or whatever movement is popular in your region? Is there skating or swimming or some other activity that is enjoyable for all ages? Is your school a real community center, or is it cut off and aloof from families? Do you have a community center at which people of all ages feel welcome?

Are there opportunities in creative and performing arts for people who are not enthusiastic about sports? It's nice if the school can afford a full-fledged music and drama department, but do we have to give up if the necessary funds aren't available? Many communities, large and small, have amateur dramatic and music groups. If the community can't afford professionals, why not encourage those amateur groups to be open and encouraging to teenagers? Again, most schools have some sort of stage facility that can be used by amateur citizen groups. It is often a question of gaining cooperation from municipal or school authorities to use them—another instance in which spirit rather than money is the key.

Is there a teen drop-in center where young people can gather in warmth, comfort, and a welcoming atmosphere? Or is there no place for teenagers in your town but the local soda shop? The latter is okay if young people are really welcome there, but it isn't so good if merchants or police are constantly dispersing the crowd that gathers to talk, laugh, and horse around. Young people are going to congregate, and the question for us is where and under what conditions.

Are there activities available that might begin to satisfy the desire for adventure, which is particularly strong during the teenage years? Young people often find adventure in doing what is forbidden. There will always be something fascinating about the forbidden, I suppose, but the amount of crime connected with it could be significantly reduced by providing challenging activities at least occasionally. What is considered challenging obviously varies from place to place and group to group, but adults can cooperate with teenagers to plan events the young people consider exciting. In one community it might be a race of some kind: bicycle, mini-bike, or jalopy. In another, it might be conquering natural phenomena such as mountains, rapids, harsh conditions.

What does your town do for young people who have had at least one brush with the law? Is there a juvenile police officer? What kind of case loads do the probation officers carry (thirty-five is the recommended limit)? Does a youngster in trouble have to get out of town? Is he or she ostracized and labeled for the rest of life? Is there real help, or only condemnation, for someone who sampled drugs or alcohol and got awfully sick? What kind of help is available?

Any one of these suggestions is of much greater importance than it might seem on the surface. These activities are important because they bring individuals or groups out of their isolation and give them a stake in the community. They are important because they bring people of all ages into continuing contact with one another. They keep communication open between young people and older people and give them a constantly renewed opportunity to learn from one another and find hope in one another. The presence or absence of such programs in a community tells us about the spirit of the place and how much the people there care about each other.

None of these questions, or the answers to them, appear to have much connection with the citizen-volunteer in corrections. They don't seem to be relevant to prisons or criminals. Actually, my questions have everything to do with criminals. It must not be forgotten that the most grisly criminal you can imagine—like the dirty old man of forty-five who murdered two men in cold blood and raped four women—was once a fine young lad with hope of happiness and fulfillment. But something went wrong, perhaps very early in his life. Maybe no one took time to notice. Perhaps people noticed, but said, "Well, it's the family he comes from. He's not our problem." And so he grew to be a criminal.

We will always have some crime, some criminals. The most conscientious community will fail with a few but there are far too many young men of eighteen, nineteen, and twenty who are already in prison and may be headed for a life of degeneracy and criminality. For some, it may be too late to do much. Some are slipping fast, and their lives may end with a policeman's bullet, or they may vegetate in prison.

The tragedy is that many of these young people could have been steered in different paths if someone had intervened a few years sooner, if their schools or communities had helped fill the yawning gaps left by their parents. The money those communities denied for youth facilities will be paid a hundred times over to keep prisons going. Prisons are far too expensive a proposition both in dollars and in lives wasted.

Youth Resource Councils

"I'm a jailor, not a miracle man," said the prison guard. "You send me your broken glass and think I'm gonna recycle it into diamonds?" Every prison guard, every judge, every policeman does at least a little complaining about the results society expects them to achieve with people who violate the law. Every expert knows that prevention of crime, though painstaking, is far better than the best cures the best criminal justice system can offer.

There's no sense in sitting about complaining that society isn't perfect; it never will be. Professionals from many disciplines offer us suggestions about how to improve our society, how to prevent crime, and it makes a lot of sense to listen and try to implement their suggestions. One of the most frequent recommendations made for preventing juvenile crime is to form youth resource councils. Some cities and towns, but not nearly enough, have followed this recommendation.

Existing youth resource councils vary considerably in size and style, but all of them are basically agencies or organizations whose purpose is to prevent young people from committing crime and to assist youngsters in trouble before their problems become too serious to be handled in the community. The council may be publicly or privately funded and operated, but in either case it is open to all who need it. It accepts referrals from official sources such as police, courts, and schools, as well as assisting individual parents with their children, and young people who simply appear on their own in search of help. The council may be big or small, relatively formal or informal, depending on the needs of a particular community. And it may exist under a variety of different names which would, hopefully, sound more appealing than the term I use here. I feel the need of apologizing for using such an awkward name, but the program was long ago given a label by a bureaucrat, and I use it only because the label has become standard.

Depending on the needs of the community, most youth resource councils have one or more functions. A council may offer short-term counseling to those who seek it and be a kind of crisis center, or it may act as a referral center only. For example, if an individual needs long-term counseling or psychiatric care, the council may refer the person to an appropriate agency which already exists in the community. The difficulty for many people is that they don't know where to go or how to find their way in the maze of bureaucratic agencies. They often get the runaround and end up with no help at all. Therefore, the council acts as an advocate and follows up on individual cases to make certain the person actually receives the necessary assistance.

In addition to handling referrals, a council may coordinate existing services, both public and private, using their facilities effectively and efficiently rather than duplicating facilities. An example of this is found in a town or city that actually has many facilities for its citizens. However, many of the organizations may be very inbred and working more toward the preservation of their own existence than for the benefit of persons in need of help. They may even be working in competition with one another and at cross-purposes, and be highly resistant to the notion of cooperating. Thus, a youngster might be talking with the mental health clinic, be in difficulty with the local police, getting one set of advice from his probation officer, another from his clergyman, and possibly a third set from the school counselor. If all these groups or persons don't work together, the child can end up confused, and worse off than if he had no official assistance. A council that can engender cooperation and coordination helps prevent this common situation.

Some councils concentrate on developing needed services in communities that have few resources. Obviously, these services can vary greatly, from the need for a remedial reading program to providing an athletic program to dealing with the problem of overcrowded living conditions. Whatever the specific need, the council can be a focal point for citizen action.

Other councils may attempt to develop new programs to help the hard-to-reach youngsters who don't belong to traditional social groups in the community. An outreach program might consist of a hot line in one town. Or it might be something a little unusual, such as the YMCA's Mini-Bike Project in Los Angeles. The mini-bike is an important phenomenon in the life of many teenagers, a powerful tool that symbolizes fun, adventure, mobility, and status. Also, it is of far greater interest to many youngsters than traditional sports activities. So, the YMCA uses a program which trains young people to ride skillfully and safely. In the process, they get a chance to talk with and reach a large number of teenagers who would normally have shunned any organized program, any boys' club, or any counseling.

Approximately one hundred cities and towns across the United States have seen the wisdom of prevention and have organized such councils in their communities. Some started because of a crisis: a teenage murder case or an epidemic of drug abuse. There is no need to wait for a crisis, and no longer a need for individual communities to struggle through the process of figuring out what constitutes a good youth council. The National Council on Crime and Delinquency has published a set of guidelines showing what a council should accomplish and giving descriptions of five kinds of councils. Each example is a little different in structure, style, and auspices.

The needs of your community may be different from those described by NCCD, but there is no single pattern which must be followed. There is no ideal to which one must conform. The council, in its design and function, should conform to only one thing: the needs of the youth in the community.

In every case cited by the NCCD, a successful youth council seemed to depend on two main assets: a small core of professionals, who were needed for planning, direction, and especially for direct counseling; and a large number of citizen volunteers, who were vitally important for several reasons. First, they were able to put their varied individual talents to use in a very meaningful way. Second, they provided a multitude of talents that no single agency could ever bring to bear. Third, they made the council a less formal, less official, less formidable place, to which many people could come for help without any stigma of disgrace or criminality. In one council in Michigan, nearly half the people who were helped by the council were either parents having difficulty with their teenagers or teenagers who dropped in to seek help in "handling their parents." They were not referred by the courts or the police or any official group. They just brought themselves to the council. This was a totally noncoercive kind of prevention which is nearly impossible to achieve through an official agency. Another community gave the elderly people of its town a new meaning and usefulness by putting them in charge of the job bureau for teenagers.

In all cases, the youth resource council, in all its varieties, increased the spirit of community by replacing condemnation with helpfulness. It does not matter exactly what form a youth council takes or what name you give it. The only thing that matters is that families and youths are served and their problems are dealt with in an open and helpful way. It helps to assure another opportunity for young people so that children who start life full of promise and hope will not have to end it in despair and disgrace. It helps all of us. Neither this nor any citizen action will eliminate all problems or failures, but it surely cannot fail to make our society much better than it now is.

Changing the Law

I must confess that there is something very important which I have neglected to say until now. I fear I may have given the impression that we can really change the world if our wills are strong and our backs firm—not the world, perhaps, but a good part of it if we work directly with our young offenders or potential delinquents. I said it all because I believe it, and I've seen much good come from such work.

But there is one thing we cannot do by working in prisons or courts or even within the limits of our own communities. We must move far beyond the community to change the laws that make criminals out of those who are not. They are sinners, perhaps, like the rest of us. Sometimes they are very unpleasant persons with revolting habits, but they are not necessarily criminals.

There is a host of laws that should be changed. There are laws that make criminals out of children who are too long truant from school, or out of sick alcoholics and drug addicts, laws that criminalize prostitutes while their customers are not penalized, and hold poor people in jail under excessive bail, laws that criminalize gambling in one state while the next state has a government-sponsored lottery, laws that permit dangerous weapons to come easily into the hands of ordinary persons, who ultimately use them on others. These examples top the list.

Our work with individual offenders is seriously hampered as long as the law permits so many inequities. To change these laws, we need volunteers who have the courage to take on a legislature, a task which also requires public education and organization, since most legislatures do nothing without sufficient pressure from constituents. It is a task which will often involve the volunteer in politics, in seeking good candidates, supporting and electing them, and weeding out bad public servants. This work demands some knowledge of the law and the inner workings of a legislature.

Trying to change the law is an extremely complex kind of work, but it can provide a marvelous challenge to the volunteer who glories in doing difficult things. It is ideal for the person who prefers to work with ideas and strategies, with organizational complexities, and with groups of people instead of individuals. Of course, this work can't be pursued alone. On the national level, the National Council on Crime and Delinquency and Common Cause are two organizations that put a great deal of energy into changing laws. They are also excellent sources of information about the multitude of state and local citizen organizations which have developed in recent years to foster change in our legal system. If you are deeply interested in the criminal-justice system, but don't feel you want to work directly with offenders, you couldn't assist in a better way than by working for greatly needed improvements in the criminal law.

Working with a legislature may seem rather remote from where we began in our discussion of prisons, but in reality it isn't. It is with the law, which is made by our political representatives, that we say what will or will not constitute a crime. It is with the law that we say what shall be the consequences for violation of criminal statutes; whether we shall have capital punishment, long prison sentences, fines, or restitution. The law is one of the most important means by which we can judge a society. It tells us whether a society is just and humane or whether it is harsh and vengeful. And it is interesting to note that the cruelty or humanity of the law in any society is almost synonymous with the conditions of cruelty or humanity in its prisons. This is why

Dostoyevsky could say, "The degree of civilization in a society can be judged by entering its prisons."

Now that you perceive our relationship with and our responsibility for the offenders of our society, isn't it time to check the organizations listed in the following pages to see where you could join the thousands of men and women now volunteering somewhere in the criminal justice system? We could talk about the problem forever, but we need people who will do something about it, people perhaps like Louis Schweitzer, the founder of the Vera Institute, mentioned in chapter 7. When Louis Schweitzer died, Nicholas B. Katzenbach delivered the following eulogy. All of us would do well to meditate on it for a while, and try to follow the example of that great man.

Louis Schweitzer believed passionately in the ability and obligation of ordinary men to make the Constitution work. He would not leave the law to lawyers and he was right. He thought that the Constitution and the Bill of Rights should mean what they said.

He thought it was morally wrong to let men rot in jail before they were tried, their families left without support, their jobs forfeited. Law professors and reformers for decades had talked about the injustices of automatic high bail based on a man's charge alone; how he ought to be released on his word if he checked out as a resident with firm ties to the community. Louis Schweitzer was the first person willing to stick his neck out and try the new way that others talked about, to invest his time and his money and his reputation in developing a fairer system.

Louis Schweitzer founded the Vera Institute of Justice, named for his mother. Vera means truth, literally, but what Louis Schweitzer stood for was commitment—personal, persevering, undaunted by "experts." That is what the criminal justice system in America needs more than anything today—citizens who care enough to put themselves on the line, to go into prisons and see what is happening to men, to devote energy, money, but most of all themselves to translating grandiose words like "rehabilitation" into something real that can make a difference to a man.

Louis Schweitzer enjoyed people and was tolerant of their failings. He was a generous man with a warm sense of humor. He was a modest man who, in his giving, always stayed in the background. There are no Lectures or Awards or Chairs or Buildings named for Louis Schweitzer. The legacy left is the thousands of human beings who have their liberty because he cared, as well as the administration of criminal justice which is more humane and has a more hopeful horizon, because he cared.

ORGANIZATIONS THAT CAN HELP THE VOLUNTEER

Alston Wilkes Society, P.O. Box 363, Columbia, S.C. 29202. Functions in South Carolina only.

American Bar Association, Committee on Crime Prevention and Control, 1155 East 60 St., Chicago, Ill. 60637. Especially useful for members of the legal profession.

American Civil Liberties Union, 22 East 40th Street, New York, New York 10016. A national organization that has offices in all states. Also see National Prison Project listing, a project of ACLU.

American Correctional Association, Committee on Citizen Participation, Woodridge Station, P.O. Box 10176, Washington, D.C. 20018. A national organization, primarily for people working in the correctional field.

American Friends Service Committee, 160 North 15th St., Philadelphia, Pa. 19102. A very active organization in prison work, the Committee has 10 regional offices, in Maryland, Massachusetts, Illinois, Ohio, Iowa, North Carolina, New York, California (2), and Washington State.

Amicus, Inc., 1141 Plymouth Building, 12 South 6 St., Minneapolis, Minn. 55402. Amicus has a very good sponsorship program, and it is very helpful about giving information to people who might want to start a similar program. The Amicus program is limited to Minnesota.

Big Brothers of America, Suburban Station Building, Philadelphia, Pa. 19103. Big Brothers do a lot of work with juveniles on probation, and they always need volunteers. A nation-wide organization with many regional offices.

Bucks County Citizens' Committee, c/o Bucks County Prison, 138 Pine St., Doylestown, Pa. 18901. This group provides a good model for prison volunteers on the county level. A letter to the group will be answered with good information on its programs.

The Children's Bureau, Department of Health, Education, and Welfare, Washington, D.C. It is a good source of information on children's problems.

The Clement Stone Foundation, WCS Center for Community and Social Concerns, Inc., 2849 West 71 St., Chicago, Ill. 60629. This group sponsors several volunteer programs in the Midwest.

Community Volunteers Project, Department of Corrections, 831 West Morgan St., Raleigh, N.C. 27603. Has an active sponsorship program.

Floating Foundation of Photography, West 79th St. Boat Basin, New York, N.Y. Excellent example of a good creative program being carried on in several New York prisons.

The Fortune Society, 1545 Broadway, New York, N.Y. 10036. One of the most active organizations working both within and outside prisons especially assisting ex-prisoners. Its work is primarily in New York and New Jersey, but it sends speakers anywhere to explain the work which needs to be done, and publishes a regular newsletter which will be sent anywhere in the country upon request.

International Halfway House Association, 2316 Auburncrest, Cincinnati, Ohio 45219.

International Prisoner's Aid Association, 436 West Wisconsin Ave., Milwaukee, Wis. 53203. Prints a directory of all prisoner-aid groups.

Job Therapy, Inc., 150 John St., Seattle, Wash. 98103. This is one of the very good volunteer programs of the country, and it will send information on the program to anyone who requests it.

John Howard Association, 608 South Dearborn St., Chicago, Ill. 60605. Another source of information.

Man to Man (M-2) Program, c/o Job Therapy, Inc., 150 John St., Seattle, Wash. 98103. Cf. Job Therapy listing above.

Middlesex County House of Correction, Director of Volunteers, Box 565, Billerica, Mass. 01821. Has one of the most extensive and varied volunteer programs found in any prison. It shares information and will respond to queries.

National Bar Association, 6326 South Cottage Grove Ave., Chicago, Ill. 60637. Now sponsoring several prison programs designed specifically for lawyer participation.

National Center for Voluntary Action, 1735 Eye St., N.W., Washington, D.C. 20006. The Center has comprehensive files on volunteer opportunities in corrections and is one of the best sources of information about local programs. There are regional offices also in New York, Chicago, Atlanta, and Los Angeles. The staff at the Center is very helpful and anxious to disseminate any information it has.

National Coordinating Council on Drug Abuse Education and Information, 1211 Connecticut Ave., N.W., Washington, D.C. 20036.

National Council of Juvenile Court Judges, University of Nevada, P.O. Box 8978, Reno, Nev. 89507.

National Council on Crime and Delinquency is the largest citizen organization in the criminal field, with state councils in nearly half the states of the country. It is a good source of information and also publishes some of the best periodical literature in the field. Write to whichever of the following regional offices is nearest your home: Eastern Regional Office, Paramus, N.J. 07652; Midwestern Regional Office, 18703 Dixie Highway, Homewood, Ill. 60430; Southern Regional Office, 508 Littlefield Building, Austin, Tex. 78701; Western Regional Office, 703 Market Street, San Francisco, Calif. 94103.

National Information Center for Volunteers in Courts, P.O. Box 2150, Boulder, Colo. 80302. Has the most comprehensive files on programs which now exist in courts and probation; also developing files on prison programs. They are the best source of information for the citizen who wants to know whether there is a program in his local court; also for those who want help in starting programs. They also have an extensive list of publications which are extremely helpful.

National Prison Project, 1424 16th Street, N.W., Suite 44, Washington, D.C. 20036.

Norfolk Fellowship, Massachusetts Correctional Institution (MCI), Box 43, Norfolk, Mass. 02056. This is a model fellowship program and is helpful to those who wish to start something similar.

Offender Aid and Restoration of Virginia, Inc. (OAR), 190 Rugby Rd., P.O. Box 3304, Charlottesville, Va. 22903. Another good program which works both in the prisons and outside, helping ex-prisoners. Operates in Virginia only.

P.A.C.E. Institute, Cook County Jail, 2600 South California Ave., Chicago, Ill. 60608. A good program and one of the best-known being conducted in jails. The institute will send information on its program.

Partners, 817 17th St., Suite 435, Denver, Colo. 80202. Works especially with juveniles and is actively cooperating with volunteer court programs.

Pre-Release Center, Beauford H. Jester Units, Richmond, Tex. 77469. Has an extensive pre-release program.

Prison Health Project, 80 Boylston St., Room 1201, Boston, Mass. 02116. This is not really a volunteer group. The role of the volunteer in the medical area is obviously limited, yet it is an area of great need in prisons. Groups like this one can be organized to survey medical facilities and services in prisons and to keep the pressure on for improvement.

Project Re-Entry, c/o Norfolk Fellowship, MCI, Box 43, Norfolk, Mass. 02056. An excellent project through which ex-inmates assist prisoners soon to be released. Information on its development is available.

Project Self-Respect, c/o Behavioral Services, Shelby County Penal Farm, Memphis, Tenn. 38128.

Project SERVE, Community Service Society of New York, 105 East 22 St., New York, N.Y. 10010. This group aims at using retired persons in community corrections and prevention work with youth. Has a directory of nationwide opportunities for older persons.

Sound, c/o Maryland House of Correction, Jessup, Md. 20794.

Theatre for the Forgotten, Inc., 106 West End Ave., New York, N.Y.

Thresholds, Inc., Dr. Milton E. Burglass, 22 Ellsworth Ave., Cambridge, Mass.

Training School for Boys, Skillman, N.J. 08558. Very extensive volunteer program. The school will send information upon request.

United States Jaycees, Correctional Programming Consultant, Box 1826, Lincoln, Nebr. 68501. Jaycees are very active in prisons and will provide a list of all the prisons in the country which have a Jaycees chapter.

The Vera Institute of Justice, 30 East 39 St., New York, N.Y. Consult the institute especially for detailed information on court-related projects.

VISTA—Volunteers in Service to America, 1200 19th St., N.W., Washington, D.C. Involved in many kinds of volunteer work, including corrections and prevention.

Volunteer Services Unit, 2127 Riverside Ave., Minneapolis, Minn. 55404. This is a model statewide prison program for volunteers. It is very well organized and is being used as a model for other states interested in developing a similar central headquarters through which volunteers can enter the system.

Volunteers in Probation, Inc., 200 Washington Square Plaza, Royal Oak, Mich. 48067. This is the original organization of volunteers in courts and probation. It is very helpful to individuals and groups who wish to start volunteer programs in courts. It is now affiliated with the National Council on Crime and Delinquency, so you can get information from either address.

Young Life Campaign, 720 West Monument, Colorado Springs, Colo. 80901. Concentrates on work with adolescents. The parent organization of groups such as Partners in Denver.

YWCA and YMCA are very active in assisting youths, whether or not they are offenders. Every state and large city has at least one Y in which volunteers can work with youth. The easiest way to locate your nearest Y is through the local phone book.

GLOSSARY OF PRISON SLANG

Baby starver One who is serving time for nonsupport.

B and E The offense of breaking and entering.

B and E man One who specializes in breaking and entering.

Benny An overcoat.

Big house A large state or federal prison or penitentiary. Also often called the big top.

Bug A burglar alarm.

Bull A regional term, especially in the south, for an officer or guard. There are yard bulls, gun bulls, etc., depending on where the officer works.

Bum beef What every man in prison says he has, an unfair conviction for something he did not do.

Bundling or *bundled* To be rendered incapable of action. May be used as a noun or a verb. It is a very vicious practice. Sometimes a fight may be settled by *bundling* a man in a blanket or sheet and beating him to death.

Busted, to be To be arrested.

Buy out, to To purchase one's way out of prison; to pay off an employee in return for an early parole.

This is quite illegal. Officials say it never happens; inmates say it does or they wouldn't have a term for it.

Candy man   A child molester.

Cannonball   A round safe; also refers to a safe which is very difficult to open.

Case, to   To look over a place before robbing it, as in *to case* the joint.

China   False teeth.

Chopper   A machine gun.

Con man   One who specializes in separating people from their money by means of trickery rather than violence.

Contract   An unwritten agreement to arrange for some person's death; i.e., murder. Used primarily in organized crime.

Cooler   A term used in some sections of the country to mean the solitary confinement cell.

Cop out, to   To plead guilty to an offense as charged.

Cop a plea, to   Another version of cop out.

Cop shop   The police station.

Crab bait   A regional term referring to a new inmate.

Crash out   An escape. May be used as a noun or a verb.

Creeping	The act of sneaking up on a person, and getting a little too close for comfort. This can provoke a violent response from inmates because they often do not feel safe with some of their fellow prisoners.
Crib	A regional term, mostly Western, meaning a safe.
Cribman	A safecracker.
Croak, to	To die. This can also refer to murderous deaths.
Croaker	A doctor.
Detainer	A request to the prison authority from any criminal-justice agency asking that the agency (e.g., police, court, parole board, etc.) be informed when the inmate in question is to be released. The inmate may have to face other charges, he may have a consecutive sentence to serve in another prison, or he may be a parole violator. Inmates who have detainers on them are generally considered security risks by prison authorities, are denied work release, furlough, or any trusty status. In many cases, the detainer system is very unfair to the prisoner.
Diddler	A child molester.
Ding, on the	Being a panhandler or a bum.
Double saw	$20.00.
Fence	One who buys stolen goods from the thief for a fraction of their real value and sells

them at a profit in what appears (at first glance) to be a legitimate business.

Fin	$5.00.
Fingerman	One who makes the decision about a crime to be committed; e.g., which place will be robbed.
Fish	A popular term for a new inmate. He may also be called a new fish.
Footpad	A mugger.
Fuzz	The police.
Gaf, gig	An unlikely story or a tall tale. May be used as a noun or a verb.
Gat	A gun.
Gate fever	The nervous tension felt by inmates just prior to release.
Hack	This can have two meanings. In some areas, it refers to an officer the inmates don't like. In others, it is a standard term for all officers.
Hat factory	A mental hospital.
Head gee	The top man or administrator, the warden.
Hide, a	A place to hide contraband; also called a *stash*.
Hit	A murder, especially one which is premeditated.

Hit man	A hired killer.
Head shrinker	Properly refers to psychiatrists, but can also refer to a whole department of psychologists and counselors.
Hoist	An armed robbery.
Hoist man	One who specializes in armed robbery.
Hole, the	Solitary confinement cell.
Hooker	A prostitute.
Hot box	A stolen car.
Ice	Diamonds.
Joint, the	Another term for the state prison. Not to be confused with *a* joint, which is marijuana.
Jug man	A bank robber, especially one who specializes in banks rather than stores or homes.
Juice	Bribe money.
Kite	When used as a noun, this refers to a letter or message taken out of the prison without the knowledge of the authorities. Especially prevalent in prisons which still have censorship. May also be used as a verb, the act of carrying the letter past.
Lam, to be on the	To be a fugitive from justice, on the run.
Lamster	A fugitive.
Lay a note, to	To shortchange a cashier.

Life on the installment plan	A series of limited prison sentences which, with persistent criminality, add up to life in prison.
Loid	A strip of celluloid used to open locks.
Loidman	One who is expert in using the loid.
Loud talker	One who deliberately talks within hearing of an officer. He is a nuisance because inmates can never be sure whether some illegal practices may be revealed as a result of his talking.
Mark, a	One who is easy to rob; e.g., an easy *mark*.
Mary ellen man	One who pick's a man's pockets while telling him a fascinating sex story.
Over the fence	The other side of the prison wall.
Paper hanger	One who passes bad checks.
Pen man	A forger.
Pete	Popular term for a safe.
Peteman	A safecracker.
Piece	A gun.
Pigeon drop	A confidence game. A wallet with money in it may be dropped near a person who looks like an easy mark. The victim is invited to share the money if he or she puts up some money to show good faith. Victim never sees any of the money again.

Piped, to be	To be hit or attacked with a lead pipe.
Plant, a	Some form of bait used by prison authorities to trap a man in an illegal activity which they may have known he was involved in, but could not prove.
Planted, to be	To be placed in solitary confinement for a long period of time.
Plea bargain	To plead guilty to a lesser offense than the one originally charged, in order to avoid the trial process, which is very time-consuming and expensive. This is very common in courts which have a large backlog of cases. In fact, the prosecutor says to the defendant, "I'll let you plead guilty to a lesser offense, and give you a short sentence, if you will save me the time and trouble of preparing a trial. If you make me go through a trial, I'll really throw the book at you." This can work favorably or unfavorably for the defendant, depending on whether he is really guilty of a serious offense, and on whether the prosecutor has very solid evidence of the serious offense.
Punk	An inmate who permits himself to be used homosexually; he is not really homosexual by nature, but submits rather than fight an older or stronger group.
Queen	An effeminate homosexual.
Rapo	A sex offender.
Right guy	Also called a good con; one who minds his own business, does his time without com-

plaint, and doesn't become involved in any prison troubles.

Riot bait	Bad food.
Rod	A gun.
Rod man	One who always uses a gun in his crimes.
Satch	A piece of linen paper soaked in heroin and dried with a hot iron. When it arrives in the prison in a letter, the inmate tears it into little bits and cooks it, taking the heroin out through a piece of cotton.
Sawbuck	$10.00.
Score	The fruits of a robbery. Can also refer to the place which is to be robbed. Inside the prison, a score may mean extra items which have been obtained by stealth; e.g., extra food stolen from the kitchen.
Score, settling a	Getting revenge.
Screw	The most popular term for officers; also used as a verb and a profanity.
Second-story man	A burglar who specializes in "upstairs" work only, places where furs, money, etc., may be hidden. He does not steal TVs or the silverware, which are located on the first floor.
Setback	Denial of parole when it was expected.
Shank	A knife.
Shingle	License plate.

Shiv	A knife.
Shrink, the	The psychiatrist.
Six *Six-four*	*Six* is the lookout man; *four* performs the illegal activity. *Six-four* is the warning given by the lookout man. It also means, "Watch out. The officer is coming."
Skimmer	A hat.
Skin beef	A sentence for a sex crime.
Skinner or *skin man*	A sex offender.
Sky pilot	A minister, priest, or rabbi.
Soup	Nitroglycerin.
Soup man	One who uses nitroglycerin to blast open safes, a special art.
Spring, to	To be released from prison, especially on bail; e.g., my brother *sprung* me.
Square John	One who is not usually involved in a life of crime; one who commits only one crime, a crime of passion, such as a murder.
Stall man	One who distracts the victim to be robbed, while his or her partner performs the robbery.
Stash	A place to hide contraband.
Sticker	A warrant or a detainer.

Stoolie or
stool pigeon An informer.

Ticket A warrant or detainer.

Tricking The process of soliciting customers for prostitution.

Typewriter A machine gun.

Wall pete A wall safe.

Warrant In this context a *warrant* is a writ issued by
a magistrate or other competent authority,
and addressed to an officer of the law requiring him to arrest the person named.

Wheel man One who drives the getaway car in a robbery.

Wire A person who has influence with the authorities.

Working the
glory road Evincing piety (e.g., regular attendance at
chapel) or reform in the hope of an early
parole.

Wrapping up Nearing the end of one's prison sentence.

Chapter 1

1. Readers may wish to obtain *Criminal Statistics,* a very interesting little booklet. It is one of a series of monographs called the Crime and Delinquency Series, published and distributed by the National Institute of Mental Health, 5600 Fishers Lane, Rockville, Md. 20852.
2. The list of federal and state institutions is compiled annually by the American Correctional Association, 4321 Hartwick Road, Suite L-208, College Park, Md. 20740.
3. *Local Jails, a Report Presenting Data for Individual County and City Jails from the 1970 National Jail Census,* carried out by the Law Enforcement Assistance Administration and the Bureau of the Census (Washington, D.C.: U.S. Government Printing Office, 1973).
4. Cressey, Donald R. (editor), *The Prison: Studies in Institutional Organization and Change* (New York: Holt, Rinehart & Winston, 1961). Refer to the entire first chapter, written by Irving Goffman, "On the Characteristics of Total Institutions: the Inmate World," pp. 15-67.
5. Refer to the *National Jail Census,* op. cit., the section on Institutional Data, pp. 160-322.
6. *The Emerging Rights of the Confined* (South Carolina Department of Corrections, 1972). Distributed by the Correctional Development Foundation, Inc., 1311 Marion Street, Columbia, South Carolina 29201. See all of chapter 4 for a detailed description of trends on the question of censorship.
7. Neil P. Cohen and Dean Hill Rivkin, "Civil Disabilities: The Forgotten Punishment," *Federal Probation,* June 1971.
8. Refer to the *Challenge of Crime in a Free Society,* the Report of the President's Commission on Law Enforcement and the Administration of Justice, chapter 2. Also see the complete *Task Force Report: Assessment of Crime* (Washington, D.C.: U.S. Government Printing Office).

9.   *Crime in the United States, Uniform Crime Reports—1971* (Washington, D.C.: U.S. Government Printing Office, 1972).

10.   Ibid., arrest data, page 115. Total recorded arrests for drunkenness were 1,804,800, making it the largest single category of arrests.

11.   *National Prisoner Statistics, State Prisoners: Admissions and Releases, 1970.* Federal Bureau of Prisons, U.S. Department of Justice, Washington, D.C. [n.d.].

12.   Sol Rubin, "Illusions of Treatment in Sentences and Civil Commitments," *Crime and Delinquency,* vol. 16 (January 1970): 79-92. The original study was done by William L. Jacks, statistician for the Pennsylvania Board of Parole, and printed in the *American Journal of Corrections,* November-December, 1957.

Chapter 2

1.   The basis for this statement is taken from an article by Milton Burdman, Deputy Director of the California Department of Corrections, written for the *Journal of the Beverly Hills Bar Association.* The reader may interpret this differently, but his statement was: "The main body of research information has produced consistent evidence that offender success rates do not vary significantly when proportions of persons granted probation increase markedly." Based on a lecture he gave, I take this to mean that there is always a small percentage of offenders who continue in crime no matter what we do with them. The problem is that we cannot know in advance which persons they will be.

Chapter 3

1.   Joint Commission on Correctional Manpower and Training, *Volunteers Look at Corrections* (Washington, D.C.: The Commission, 1969).

2. According to the National Jail Census of 1970, about one-fourth of the nation's jails do not even have flush toilets in the cells.
3. Sue Opipare, Peggy Porter, and Ida Reed, "Breaking Into Jail," *Library Journal*, September 15, 1971, pp. 2734-36.
4. Copies of the May 1973 issue of *Fortune News*, a publication of the Fortune Society (mentioned in chapter 2), were returned from the federal penitentiary in Leavenworth, Kansas, stamped "Not authorized at U.S. Penitentiary."

Chapter 4

1. Interesting examples of such disciplinary reports can be found in a book by Gresham M. Sykes, *The Society of Captives: A Study of a Maximum Security Prison* (Princeton, N.J.: Princeton University Press, 1958). Though this book was written several years ago, it remains one of the outstanding studies of the inmate social system and the roles played by prisoners and guards. It is a must on the reading list of anyone who plans to volunteer in a prison.
2. Recently, I accidentally met Neil on the street, tentatively inquired about his current activities, and was informed he was "studying for the Ph.D. at Harvard." I didn't check out the truth of his statement, but it wouldn't surprise me in the least.

Chapter 5

1. For further information on this aspect of prison life for women, the reader may want to read David A. Ward and Gene G. Kassebaum, *Women's Prison: Sex and Social Structure* (Chicago: Aldine Publishing Co., 1965).
2. Ben H. Bagdikian, *The Shame of the Prisons* (New York: Pocket Books, 1972), pp. 82-83.
3. Ward and Kassebaum, op. cit.

Chapter 6

1. In Re Gault, 387 U.S. 1 (1967).
2. James, Howard, *Children in Trouble: A National Scandal* (New York: David McKay Company, 1969).

Chapter 7

1. *The Challenge of Crime in a Free Society*, the report of the President's Commission on Law Enforcement and the Administration of Justice (Washington, D.C.: U.S. Government Printing Office, 1967). See the entire chapter 5, on the Courts. You might also want to look at the complete *Task Force Report on the Courts*, of which chapter 5 of the final report is a summary. The Task Force Reports are also available from the Government Printing Office.
2. From a speech of Dr. Ernest L. V. Shelley, Chief Psychologist, Lansing, Michigan, Juvenile Court, to the National Conference of Volunteers in Probation, October 4-7, 1970.
3. Joe Alex Morris, *First Offender* (New York: Funk and Wagnalls, 1971), pp. 115-130.
4. *The Challenge of Crime in a Free Society*, p. 166.
5. Address of C. E. Hughes to the New York State Bar Association, 42nd Annual Meeting, 1919.
6. John Augustus, *A Report of the Labors of John Augustus for the Last Ten Years in the Aid of the Unfortunate* (Boston: Wright & Hasty Printers, 1852), p. 5.
7. Ibid., p. 23.
8. Taken from a letter written by Mary Pickman and printed in the *VIP Examiner*, a newsletter of Volunteers in Probation, Winter 1973, p. 1.
9. *Programs in Criminal Justice Reform*, the Ten-Year Report (1961-1971) of the Vera Institute of Justice, pp. 31-33.

BIBLIOGRAPHY

American Correctional Association, *Directory of Juvenile and Adult Correctional Institutions and Agencies,* updated annually; compiled by the American Correctional Association, 4321 Hartwick Road, Suite L-208, College Park, Maryland 20740.

Bagdikian, Ben H., *The Shame of the Prisons* (New York: Simon and Schuster, Pocket Books, 1972).

Barnes, Henry E., and Megley K. Teeters, *New Horizons in Criminology,* 3rd edition (Englewood Cliffs, New Jersey: Prentice-Hall, 1959).

Blake, James, *The Joint* (New York: Doubleday & Company, 1971).

Brown, Claude, *Manchild in the Promised Land* (New York: New American Library, Signet, 1971).

Callaghan, Dean P., *Directory of State, Regional, National and International Planners and Coordinators of Volunteer Programs in Corrections* (Boulder, Colorado: National Information Center for Volunteers in Courts, 1972).

Citizen Action to Control Crime and Delinquency (Paramus, New Jersey: National Council on Crime and Delinquency, 1968). A pamphlet describing fifty citizen projects. Available from NCCD, Paramus, New Jersey.

Clark, Ramsey, *Crime in America* (New York: Simon and Schuster, 1970).

Cleaver, Eldridge, *Soul on Ice* (New York: McGraw-Hill Book Company, 1968).

Cressey, Donald P., *Other People's Money* (New York: The Free Press, 1953).

deFord, Miriam Allen, *Stone Walls: Prisons from Fetters to Furloughs* (Philadelphia: Chilton Books, 1962).

De Rhram, Edith, *How Could She Do That? A Study of the Female Criminal* (New York: Clarkson N. Potter, Inc., 1969).

Directory of Halfway Houses, available from International Halfway House Association; for address, see list of organizations.

Directory of Law Student in Correction Programs, available from the National Council on Crime and Delinquency, Paramus, New Jersey.

Directory of Prisoner's Aid Agencies, available from International Prisoners Aid Association; for address, see list of organizations.

Giallombardo, Rose, *Society of Women: A Study of a Women's Prison* (New York: John Wiley and Sons, 1966).

Glaser, Daniel, *The Effectiveness of a Prison and Parole System* (Indianapolis: The Bobbs-Merrill Company, 1966).

Glueck, Sheldon, and Eleanor T., *Five Hundred Delinquent Women* (New York: Alfred A. Knopf, 1934). A classic study of female offenders.

Goffman, Erving, *Asylums* (Garden City, New York: Doubleday & Company, Anchor Books, 1961). An analysis of the quality of life in total institutions.

Griswold, Jack H., et al., *An Eye for an Eye* (New York: Holt, Rinehart & Winston, 1970).

Henry, Jules, *Pathways to Madness* (New York: Random House, 1965). An anthropologist's intensive study of five problem families and the complexity of the family relationship which led to emotional breakdown. Very helpful in gaining a deeper understanding of the effect of family life on the development of children.

Hough, John T., Jr., *A Peck of Salt: A Year in the Ghetto* (Boston: Little, Brown & Co., 1970). Not specifically concerned with crime, but with the ghetto conditions which breed it. A VISTA Volunteer's sensitive and beautiful account of his ghetto experience and the youngsters who were part of his life.

James, Howard, *Children in Trouble: A National Scandal* (New York: David McKay Company, 1969). A *Christian Science Monitor* reporter's evaluation of what happens to youths in trouble with the law. Excellent overview of their treatment and good introduction to juvenile delinquency for the prospective volunteer.

Katz, Sanford N., *When Parents Fail: The Law's Response to Family Breakdown* (Boston: Beacon Press, 1971).

Klare, Hugh J., editor, *Changing Concepts in Crime and Its Treatment* (Elmsford, New York: Pergamon Press, 1966). An excellent little book of essays dealing with the nature of crime and our attitudes toward criminals.

Loeser, Herta, *Women, Work, and Volunteering* (Boston: Beacon Press, 1974).

Maine, Sir Henry Sumner, *Ancient Law* (London: John Murray, 1883). An old, but valid, history of the development of ancient law prior to the written codes.

Malcolm X, *The Autobiography of Malcolm X* (New York: Grove Press, 1964). The story of ghettos, delinquency, and the rise of a revolutionary movement, which should be appreciated by all correctional volunteers.

Menninger, Karl, *The Crime of Punishment* (New York: Viking Press, 1968).

Mitford, Jessica, *Kind and Usual Punishment: The Prison Business* (New York: Alfred A. Knopf, 1973).

Morris, Joe Alex, *First Offender: A Volunteer Program for Youth in Trouble* (New York: Funk & Wagnalls, 1970).

Norman, Sherwood, *The Youth Service Bureau: A Brief Description with Five Current Programs* (Paramus, New Jersey: National Council on Crime and Delinquency, 1970).

Perlman, Robert, and David Jones, *Neighborhood Service Centers* (Washington, D.C.: U.S. Government Printing Office, U.S. Department of Health, Education, and Welfare, 1967).

Pound, Roscoe, *Criminal Justice in America* (New York: Henry Holt & Co., 1930). Excellent explanation of the development of the American system of justice and our English legal heritage.

Powers, Edwin, *Crime and Punishment in Early Massachusetts 1620-1692: A Documentary History* (Boston: Beacon Press, 1966). A very well-documented work which gives the flavor of early criminal justice, as well as an accurate history.

President's Commission on Law Enforcement and the Administration of Justice, *The Challenge of Crime in a Free Society*

(Washington, D.C.: U.S. Government Printing Office, 1967). To date, the most comprehensive report on our system of justice. Correctional volunteers should be familiar with its contents.

Richette, Lisa Aversa, *The Throwaway Children* (Philadelphia: J. B. Lippincott Co., 1969). A former Assistant D.A., handling juvenile cases, describes the horrors of the lives of youngsters she saw coming through the courts.

Rothman, David J., *The Discovery of the Asylum* (Boston: Little, Brown & Company, 1971). An excellent history of the development of modern institutions, with a special chapter on the growth of penitentiaries.

Rubin, Sol, *The Law of Criminal Corrections* (St. Paul, Minnesota: West Publishing Company, 1963). An invaluable aid in understanding the legal aspects of the correctional system.

Sands, Bill, *My Shadow Ran Fast* (Englewood Cliffs, New Jersey: Prentice-Hall, 1964).

Scheier, Ivan H., et al., *Guidelines and Standards for the Use of Volunteers in Correctional Programs* (Washington, D.C.: U.S. Department of Justice, LEAA, 1972). A comprehensive guide to volunteer program management. A must for every director of volunteers.

————, and James D. Jorgensen, *Volunteer Training for Courts and Corrections* (Metuchen, New Jersey: The Scarecrow Press, 1973). An absolute essential for the director of volunteers.

Schur, Edwin M., *Crimes Without Victims—Deviant Behavior and Public Policy: Abortion, Homosexuality, Drug Addiction* (Englewood Cliffs, New Jersey: Prentice-Hall, 1964).

————, *Our Criminal Society* (Englewood Cliffs, New Jersey: Prentice-Hall, 1969).

South Carolina Department of Corrections, *The Emerging Right of the Confined* (distributed by the Correctional Development Foundation, Inc., 1311 Marion Street, Columbia, South Carolina 20201).

Sykes, Gresham M., *The Society of Captives: A Study of a Maximum Security Prison* (Princeton, New Jersey: Princeton University Press, 1958). A classic descriptive study of the inmate social system, the roles played by prisoners and guards. Very readable, very accurate.

U.S. Government Printing Office, *Using Volunteers in Court Settings* (available from the Superintendent of Documents, Washington, D.C. 20402). A how-to guidebook for anyone planning or directing a volunteer program in a court.

Vera Institute, *Programs in Criminal Justice Reform* (the Ten-Year Report (1961-1971) of the Vera Institute of Justice, 30 East 39th Street, New York, New York).

Ward, David A., and Gene G. Kassebaum, *Women's Prison: Sex and Social Structure* (Chicago: Aldine Publishing Company, 1965). One of the few studies available on female prisoners. Emphasis on homosexuality and conformity to the inmate code.